The Responsible Methodologist

The Responsible
Methodologist
Inquiry, Truth-Telling, and Social Justice

Aaron M. Kuntz

Routledge
Taylor & Francis Group

LONDON AND NEW YORK

First published 2015 by Left Coast Press, Inc.

Published 2016 by Routledge
2 Park Square, Milton Park, Abingdon, Oxon OX14 4RN
711 Third Avenue, New York, NY 10017, USA

Routledge is an imprint of the Taylor & Francis Group, an informa business

Library of Congress Cataloging-in-Publication Data:

Kuntz, Aaron M.
  The responsible methodologist : inquiry, truth-telling, and social justice / Aaron M. Kuntz.
    pages cm
  Includes bibliographical references and index.
  ISBN 978-1-61132-368-9 (hardback : alk. paper)
  ISBN 978-1-61132-369-6 (pbk. : alk. paper)
  ISBN 978-1-61132-370-2 (institutional ebook)
  ISBN 978-1-61132-734-2 (consumer ebook)
  1. Methodology. 2. Research—Methodology. 3. Qualitative research—Methodology.
4. Learning and scholarship. I. Title.
  BD241.K827 2015
  001.4—dc23

                                                                              2015016734

ISBN 978-1-61132-368-9 hardback
ISBN 978-1-61132-369-6 paperback

To Ashley, with love (and avocados) . . .

Contents

Acknowledgements

I would like to thank the University of Alabama for giving me the time and support to work on this book. This text would not have happened without the sabbatical leave afforded me by the university as well as the intellectual companionship I have enjoyed over the years as faculty in the College of Education. I also thank those graduate students who took my special topics seminars in qualitative inquiry the past few years—these students pushed me to further refine my thoughts in important areas as I actively worked out sections of this book in class discussions and hallway conversations.

I remain thankful for the International Congress of Qualitative Inquiry, the American Educational Studies Association, the American Educational Research Association, and the Southeast Philosophy of Education Society. The annual meetings for these associations offered a space for me to try out elements of this book within a community of passionate, politically engaged scholars.

I will forever be indebted to Mitch Allen of Left Coast Press, Inc. who saw value in this project from its early stages of formation and reminded me that mine was "a good book that deserves to get even better." Quite simply, I am not sure this project would have ever come to completion were it not for my "check-in" meetings and e-mails with Mitch.

Many thanks to Kelly Guyotte for her artistic work on the icon that begins each chapter. I thank Michelle Wooten for her help composing the bibliography.

I also thank Ashley Floyd for reminding me what strong philosophical scholarship looks like and for holding my hand on long walks as we debated the finer points of engaged educational work, academic activism, and a belief in positive social change in the years to come.

And lastly I would like to thank my three children, Anna, Oscar, and Ollie, for their generative presence in my life and for teaching me what it means to be an engaged (and playful) citizen of our world.

Chapter 1

Introduction

Introduction

Peruse any academic bookstore these days or the multitude of publishers' flyers that end up in faculty mailboxes each week, and you are apt to encounter an inordinate number of texts devoted to the act of research. These books likely range from how-to manuals or step-by-step research guides to more philosophically inclined arguments regarding the role of inquiry within our contemporary society. Given the wide range of the methodological field in contemporary times, I suppose I should begin by answering questions of why *this* book and why *now*?

I came to think through this book because I was disheartened by the ease with which methodological discussions transitioned into questions of procedure. Alongside the procedurization of select methods as more legitimate than others came a disquieting parallel—that these procedural discussions governed questions of methodological responsibility and ethics. This is to say that, at times, our heightened concern with method in the academy unnecessarily constrains considerations for responsible research, and it all becomes understood in relation to overarching anxieties regarding which method to use, where to use it, and how to interpret the data it produces. Methodological responsibility, in this case, becomes reduced to maintaining the integrity of research procedure, of locating a degree of congruency of procedure. Further, methodological identity seems to draw meaning from the ability to most efficiently and effectively employ select

The Responsible Methodologist: Inquiry, Truth-Telling, and Social Justice, by Aaron M. Kuntz, 11–30.

methods—expertise as the management of procedure. The result is, to borrow from Foucault (2010), a methodologist who can "punish you like a judge and cure you like a physician" (379). In this sense methodologists may pass judgment ("the data support these claims, but not those") and play a curative role ("you tell me your concerns, and I'll prescribe a series of methods to get you the data you need"). This book begins with the premise that such positionings are, at best, misplaced. Perhaps more starkly stated, such limited considerations of responsibility and identity are dangerous.

There is a well-worn quote from Michel Foucault that addresses his motivation to engage in critique with the hope for progressive social change. In an interview Foucault (1983) notes,

> My point is not that everything is bad, but that everything is dangerous, which is not exactly the same as bad. If everything is dangerous, then we always have something to do. So my position leads not to apathy but to a hyper- and pessimistic activism. I think that the ethico-political choice we have to make every day is to determine which is the main danger. (231)

So it is that the procedurization of method and redefinition of the methodologist as someone whose expertise derives from the management of methodological technologies is dangerous. Further, such circumstances, entangled as they are within a globalized neoliberalism, reveal larger sociopolitical circumstances that require sustained critique: "we always have something to do." I follow Foucault's stance of "hyper- and pessimistic activism" that infers the progressive possibilities inherent in critical inquiry as well as the "ethico-political choice" to address select dangers. In this sense this book represents my own decision to intervene within the dangers of what I have come to term a *logic of extraction*; a historically laden normalizing rationale that promotes values of distance, fixity, and procedural ways of knowing and coming to know.

The fixation on method above all else prompted me to search for alternative discussions of inquiry. I sought ways to consider research as more than a series of neat steps but, instead, as an inquiry process that affects both what we know and how we live our lives. This brought me to Michel Foucault's (2001, 2010, 2011, 2015) work on responsibility and ethics, in particular his interpretation of *parrhesia*, and I began to work through the many ways in which inquiry itself was inevitably a political act—whether we reinscribe the normalizing processes of our present or challenge the legitimacy of commonsensical inquiry, methodological work is inevitably political. Hence the possibility that is this book.

These concerns regarding the place of inquiry in our formations of being and doing might seem a bit forced given the gravity of our contemporary contexts. At present we seem on the verge of an overlapping array of catastrophes—from rising sea levels and global warming, to ethnic conflict on every continent, to growing crises in mental illness, to social depression and anxiety, and a cultural over-reliance on pharmaceutical intervention, ours is a time of violence of multiple scales and intensities. Though I do not pretend that reconsiderations regarding inquiry and responsibility will immediately change any of these ongoing tragedies, I also refuse to believe they are completely divorced from them. We have, for example, long treated the environment as a commodity—something to be parceled out, owned, bought, and sold for individual profit. I have no doubt that this consumerist way of thinking has contributed to the accelerated degradation of our natural resources and ever-intensifying environmental catastrophes.[1] At the same time, I also believe that extending this logic of consumerism to our research approaches—that, for example, research produces data that might be interpreted within an academic market—has a decidedly negative effect on what research can do and, importantly, how we might come to know and be differently. This is to say that, for me anyway, there is not much distance at all between how we live, who we claim to be, and how we come to know; inquiry processes are forever productively entangled in the development of ontology, identity, and epistemology. Changing how we think about and enact inquiry necessarily involves changing how we interpret and act within the world; therein lies the possibility for productive social change.

Further, I have noticed in both the graduate classes I teach and engagements with colleagues throughout the academy a developing skill of supposed neutrality. This is to say that our contemporary mode of schooling seems most adept at training students to sit on the fence when it comes to questions of politics and research. By the time they make their way into graduate school, students seem quite able to point to other scholars' assertions without claiming or invoking their own. This seems strikingly apparent in the social sciences and the field of education.[2] The danger of this phenomenon, of course, is that one simply takes on the assertions of others without interrogation and, in the context of methodology, employs particular research approaches without due consideration to the sociopolitical ramifications of such practices. Methodologies necessarily bring with them select assumptions about knowing and being—perspectives on the world that are heavy with political weight.

Political involvement is a skill—one required of any engaged democracy—and I find the relationship between politics and inquiry to be (wonderfully) entangled. Our contemporary context of multiple and overlapping social crises requires a thoughtful, engaged citizenry; we do our students no favors by training them to parrot the assertions of others, be they methodological or otherwise. Our times require engaged researchers who can openly articulate the link between the work they do, the methodologies to which they subscribe, and the type of social change they envision. This is, of course, no easy task. Consequently, mine is a request that we teach and engage in inquiry differently from how we have in the past. This begins with an interrogation of the logics and rationale that inform our inquiry practices, a refusal to acquiesce to the standardization of method and those sociopolitical assumptions that inform such traditional research approaches.

Specifically in the case of educational inquiry, I share Kuhn's concern that often "researchers adopt certain methodological stances and employ particular methods, but without much awareness of why, apart from reasons of the most mechanical or 'calculative' kind" (2008, 181). In this sense the given *rationale* for methodological choice is unnecessarily technocratic, creating a self-perpetuating cycle: "mechanical" justifications encourage methodologies that are overtly mechanistic and context independent (the machinery of method can be picked up—extracted—from one context and employed in another with technical efficiency), which, in turn, privilege technocratic rationalities as a common-sensical means for making sense of our methodologies.

I might push Kuhn's thinking a bit here to further assert that in order to give anything more than a superficial reading of *why* such methods are (or should be) employed, we need to understand *how* such methods gained common-sensical traction—what logics make them visible, an option for the researcher? More importantly, what values and beliefs inform their practices? Thus, *methodological responsibility* extends from, in some way, refusing to simply implement select methods in favor of more philosophical considerations for how such methods came to be and the very material implications of employing them in select material contexts. Historicizing our methodological approaches goes a long way toward reconnecting them to particularly material political contexts; it refuses any assertions of select methodologies existing across time and space. Beyond critical moves to historicize methods—showing their necessary entanglement in sociopolitical contexts—such a sense of responsibility also entails an articulated vision for alternative spaces of possibility, places where we might act and be as other than we currently are. In this way both the past and future are brought into the present with the aim of productive social critique. Often such spaces of possibility extend from the recognition that previously legitimated forms of knowing and being (epistemological and ontological assumptions, respectively) misrepresent others' lived realities. This misrepresentation leads critical methodologists to necessarily abandon traditional forms of knowing and being in favor of more disruptive assumptions regarding the goals and practices of inquiry, perhaps even questioning the emphasis on representation all together.

As an example, in his critical ethnography *Shelter Blues,* Robert Desjarlais (1997) examines the problematics of traditional representations of *experience* and the subsequently linear narratives of meaning-making that align with their production. Desjarlais remains suspicious of experience's role in the easy production of truth as well as those standardized methods through which such coherent truth is known and articulated. In response, Desjarlais takes a Deleuzian approach to inquiry that employs a "zig-zagging" (10) methodology, one that wanders as much as it progresses. In this way Desjarlais seeks to link the articulation of his findings—his process of truth-telling—with the theoretical orientations that inform his work. In some ways this is risky methodological behavior. By not adhering to normative processes of inquiry or standardized forms of narrative, Desjarlais risks his relation to his reader and the academic field of which he is a citizen. Refusing the standardized norms of any field often results in questions regarding one's legitimacy or placement within the field in the first place: "If you aren't engaging recognizably anthropological practices of research, how can you claim a position as an anthropologist?" And yet this critical orientation, risky though it might be, is certainly productive—making available newly dynamic engagements with questions of experience, meaning-making, and material realities.

Mine, like Desjarlais's, is a wandering analysis, one that zig-zags among issues of *truth-telling, extraction, materialism, and responsibility.* In some ways this book is traditionally fashioned—holding to the linear formation of a logic and analysis that builds on itself toward a layered insight—while in other ways I strive to resist this production of tradition, to disrupt this normative element of meaning-making. The aim of my analysis takes cues from the work of Deleuze and Guattari (1988) to, in a very real sense, make methodology "stutter"—to make what has become methodological common sense no longer easy nor sensible. Mine is an interest in methodological approaches that operate among uncertain and shifting material relations, necessarily risking the very identities of those who inquire and the inquiry project as a whole.

Overview of the Book

Throughout this book I call to question traditionally distanced inquiry mechanisms even as I interrogate processes of "data analysis" and normative

Relationality, Risk, Citizenship

conceptualizations of "risk" and "truth-telling" in qualitative inquiry. In response to distancing analytical processes, I advocate for a materialist approach to inquiry, one that necessarily troubles a *logic of extraction* that predominates research practices in the field of education. Throughout I take seriously Foucault's (2011) notion of *parrhesia*, or truth-telling, and consider its relation to materialist inquiry. Foucault's explication of *parrhesia* emphasizes three important elements—each foreshadowed by my overview of Desjarlais's work: *relationality, risk,* and *citizenship,* terms certainly important for my own work as a critically engaged and politically minded methodologist. As such, I return often to these terms throughout this book, striving to understand how they might enable a productive rethinking of methodological work.

My hope is to, like Bennett (2010), offer both critiques of contemporary formations of methodological responsibility and alternatives for responsibly engaging in inquiry. As Bennett writes, "The point … is that we need both critique and positive formulations of alternatives, alternatives that will themselves become the objects of later critique and reform" (xv). In the spirit of productive critique, I engage with Foucault's interpretation of *parrhesia* to both problematize contemporary formations of methodological responsibility and to point to newly possible orientations toward inquiry as truth-telling. *Parrhesiastic* orientations to inquiry are by no means above reproach or outside critique; they are, however, a useful alternative to the traditional research methods that have come to dominate education and the social sciences.

The second element of Bennett's statement—that of "positive formulations of alternatives"—remains important yet, I fear, will inevitably produce incomplete results. Through this book I call for alternative enactments of truth-telling in our methodological work: I ask the social-justice minded inquirer to perform the role of the *parrhesiast.* As I hope to show, *parrhesia* is not about prescribed methods or certain practices; it is about an orientation to truth-telling, a becoming-with the very truths one seeks to speak. As such, I cannot point to one scholar or another and say, "This person is a *parrhesiast*" or "that text is a product of *parrhesia.*" What I can do, however, is offer a series of tentative examples that touch on the blurry edges of *parrhesiastic* work. This stems from my attempt to call for methodological work that has yet to be, the formation of a responsible methodological turn that maps out to the as-yet unknown. Ultimately, the examples given in this book will fail the test of full or complete description. It is simply my hope that theirs is a productive failure.

Through this book I seek to productively engage with the disappointment and frustration I have come to associate with the methodological landscape when it comes to questions of responsibility and ethics. In many ways it has felt as though discussions regarding what it means to be methodologically responsible were oddly divorced from methodological practice itself, as though ethical questions of practice were distanced from the inquiry practices that made methodologies most visible. As an engaged scholar, I have particular distaste for research that situates the *researched* "out there"—away from the safety of the disengaged *researcher*. Instead, I strive for practices that consider inquiry (and the inquirer) as relationally bound to the phenomenon of interest. As a necessary consequence, then, one can never fully distance oneself from either what one seeks to research or—important to this book's focus—the means by which one engages in inquiry. To be methodologically responsible, it would seem, is to recognize the entangled intersections among the what, who, how, and why of inquiry. This is ethically important and political work.

Within the field of education I often distinguish between "studying" and "working with" schools and teachers, a differentiation also claimed by Denzin and Giardina, who emphasize "working *with,* rather than conducting research *on,* communities" (2014, 19). It seems that the vast majority of school districts located near research universities suffer a great deal of "research fatigue," as graduate students and faculty seek to study teachers, classrooms, students, pedagogical practices, and so forth that are conveniently located nearby. As one local teacher recently told me, "I'm tired of being studied. Work with me—that's all I ask." Working with these same groups of educators requires a different level of commitment and, I argue, presents important distinctions to considerations of *methodological responsibility.*

Researching or *studying* others (be they people, places, curricula, etc.) invokes a position of distance with corresponding effects on how we understand responsibility. One might responsibly invoke research practices, for example, that *maintain* distance. If one were studying peer-interactions in the classroom, one might question whether to intervene when witnessing bullying behavior among an otherwise unsupervised group of students. The scenario might develop thusly: a researcher witnesses bullying and considers this occurrence as *data*—a sequence of events s/he considers meaningful and worthy of further study. Once the specter of data is cast upon any event, it may then be protected (some might say held hostage) by a host of methodological practices all aimed at maintaining a sense of purity or internal integrity. The researcher might then consider the implications of intervening within the bullying scenario on his/her data.[3] What were to happen if s/he were to "close the gap" invoked by terminology, such as "researching others"? How might it take away from the research project at hand? As the researcher considers such circumstances in light of their impact on data, the very real and material impact of bullying is,

(handwritten margin notes: "My Play shows result of working with Imagine Relationality Teacher With Scholar", "A", "Value Student / responded X")

in effect, sidelined in favor of a consistent foregrounding of methodological responsibility in the production of data.

   Though I would hope that we all would intervene—research project or not—were we to witness bullying, the distancing invoked by researching or studying others might give one pause, especially as one considers the potential impact of such nondistanced intervention on the research practice. This is not a particularly useful pause, as it turns one's energies *away* from the problematic of bullying and *toward* a fixation on research purity. Or consider for a moment the problematic of a recent dissertation project I encountered dealing with individuals enduring chronic pain. Following a series of in-depth interviews and engaged encounters with participants, the student received notice that one individual who took part in the study was hospitalized due to his/her condition. Upon hearing that the student went and made solitary vigil at the individual's bedside, a committee member shared her concern: "How could you do that? You've just jeopardized all your data, all your findings. How can I trust your conclusions as valid? You must maintain your role as a researcher—remember that."

   "When," I asked in return, "did research necessitate a loss of humanity, of being human?" The point here is that the distancing involved in studying others unnecessarily aligns issues regarding responsibility with more procedural concerns; very real issues become crowded out by a methodological fixation on maintaining the distance of research.

   A differently engaged orientation of *working with* re-imagines responsibility as contextually situated and relationally aligned. Hence, given the first example, witnessing acts of bullying requires in this case one to consider responsibility as it extends from an engaged relation, a working-with that refuses to foreground the procedural in favor of an emphasis on a relationally informed ethics of everyday engagement.[4] Similarly the dissertation student might consider the ethic of care as her responsibility as she related with the chronic pain of those she engages via inquiry. Data in these cases are never externally situated, never in need of protection from the imprint of relational context.

   As such, my aim in this book is to sketch out this relationally engaged approach and, ultimately, ask: What does it mean to be methodologically responsible given emergent ontological and epistemological assumptions about our world? Further, how might a materialist engagement with educational inquiry offer particular possibilities for methodological activism? In my reading, methodological responsibility and inquiry-as-activism exist in dynamic relation—the one informing the other in particularly productive ways. As a consequence, traditional frames for understanding responsible inquiry outside issues of social justice are no longer relevant. Inquiry-for-social-justice inherently requires

Responsibility
Permission from Authors

newly formed ethical questions. And, of course, these are always political questions that, in turn, inform the political practices of inquiry.

With such contextual developments as a backdrop, I turn to a critique in Chapter 2 of what I term a *logic of extraction*, a governing logic that foregrounds particular ways of knowing and coming to know. I locate extractive logics as informing and extending from our contemporary context of a globalized neoliberalism, with particular consequences for normative assumptions about what research can and should do, as evidenced by the two examples given above. The pervasiveness of this rationale encourages particular methodological stances, practices, and identities seen, for example, in the simplistic collapse of method and technique as the rational tools of the methodological expert. Logics of extraction most often result in an unnecessary foreclosure on the otherwise provocative possibilities of critical inquiry. In this way inquiry in the name of social justice loses its transformative potential. We exchange the possibility of progressive social change for the rather benign procedural alterations that merely re-articulate the status quo. In the face of this, I consider my own responsibility to refuse the status of methodologist-as-technocrat (as dreamy as such an identity might be) in favor of a becoming methodology with roots in materialism. Chapter 3 thus examines the implications of materialism on methodology and methodological responsibility, paying particular attention to the possibilities inherent in what has recently been termed the *critical* or *new materialism* in social theory. The materialist perspective offers relational formations of knowing and being that can never be fully severed from the material contexts from which they extend. As a consequence, materialist inquiry emphasizes the fluid movement of relations, yet does so without the impulse to capture or otherwise freeze relationality.

From this critical perspective, methodological responsibility is productively entwined in activities of risk and truth-telling, what some philosophers have termed *parrhesia*, a key term explicated in Chapter 4, perhaps the central chapter of this book. In my view *parrhesia* productively intersects with principle tenets of new materialism even as it foregrounds an engaged form of methodology as social justice work. As a consequence of the *parrhesiastic* perspective, responsible methodological work necessarily intersects with principles of social justice, refusing the extractions offered by contemporary rationalities that maintain the status quo. In Chapter 5 I end with an appreciation of hopeful and materially situated methodological wandering, practices that refuse to be claimed by the normative methodologist and dwell, instead, in the possibility of socially just and methodologically responsible practices. In the end mine is a call for methodological responsibility and risk that draws from politically engaged

, critical theories that have come to drive our analyses—methodological practice as social justice work.

As a grounding thread throughout this text I link theoretical considerations to methodological practices in two overlapping conceptual fields: embodiment and critical geography. Inquiry projects that consider embodiment and utilize a critical geographical orientation usefully reveal key tensions regarding methodological responsibility and risk. In particular, both offer distinctly materialist interpretations of meaning-making even as they require methodologists to take seriously the means by which they engage in the world in which they live. Specifically I consider embodiment and critical geography according to the following overarching tenets (referenced here and developed further throughout the chapters of this book): materialist considerations of embodiment and a critical geographical insistence on processual thinking, a relational understanding of knowing and being, privileging a critical engagement with the social world, refusing the status quo in an attempt to intervene in systems of oppression and exploitation, overt political work, and, as an extension, a desire for progressive social change. These basic tenets require much of the methodologist and, importantly, proffer select challenges and definitions for what it means to be methodologically responsible in our inquiry projects even as they require a degree of (at times, uncomfortable) risk. My aim in foregrounding questions of embodiment and critical geography is not to require that readers take on these inquiry orientations (though, of course, that would be fine as well) but instead to ground theoretical considerations within select examples and daily methodological practices.

In my desire to explode notions of methodology, responsibility, and relation, I perhaps follow the work of Pearce and MacLure, who advocate for approaches to inquiry that "create concepts, open them up, find new possibilities rather than adopt reductionist strategies that would see concepts pinned down or defined" (2009, 264). In many ways this goes against the traditional epistemological practices articulated in methodological textbooks; often coding strategies, for example, seek to reduce the number of codes in order to better define or establish some "truth" of the project, the nailing down of meaning as opposed to its opening up. So mine is a project in search of new possibilities—considerations for methodological responsibility as an opening or becoming and inquiry practice as endlessly productive.

Clarifications

It seems important to pause here and articulate a few clarifying statements. Readers will note that I spend more time talking about *embodiment* and *emplacement* throughout this text than focusing on questions concerning the *body* or *place*. This is intentional. I do not substitute one term for the other, as I believe they point to very different things. I discuss embodiment because I am most interested in issues concerning social processes, practices, and events. Though certainly concerns regarding the body are important, my sense for relational materiality is that the body mediates experience/human meaning-making. This is to say that the body is not simply a thing—discussions centered on questions of "what is the/a body?" often move with uncomfortable speed to a fixation on defining (and containing) the body with particular definitions. Similarly, I am not invested in fixing place; instead, I follow the principle tenets of critical geography and corresponding concerns for the intersection of local context and more global discourses in the production of place—place as imbued within dynamic processes of meaning-making and being. Again, it is not that these questions of bodies and places are unimportant but rather that they are not the focus of this book. I am interested instead in a relational materiality, a perspective that foregrounds processes and practices over mechanisms of containment and stasis.

Readers will also note my continual critique of *logics of extraction*. Through this critique I remain invested in disentangling the logic or rationale that foregrounds extractivist practices of knowing and coming to know, particularly within the realm of methodology. More than simply saying that all meaning-making is a form of extraction, my critique extends from a dedication to recenter the role of materiality in how we come to know. This is to say that some forms of understanding are not simply extracted ways of knowing—our embodied and emplaced experiences collude with the material world in the production of meaning: We are more than our extractions. We are relational. We have material experiences.

This concern with processual analyses—as seen in my discussion of embodiment and emplacement—set alongside a critique of extrativist rationalities, drives my interrogation of *methodological responsibility* and *risk*. It is my hope that disentangling what we know and how we come to know will make possible new ways of knowing and being that are not dependent on traditional epistemological and ontological formations. This is, of course, challenging work—though it is also, I think, hopeful work. It is a productive consequence of our existence that the rational systems that drive our meaning-making can never fully make sense of the totality of our relational lives; attempts at meaning-making inevitably fall short. There lie pivotal gaps in how we come to know the world in which we live. Out of such interstices new ways of knowing and being are possible. And yet investigating such possibility is inherently risky—challenging the very systems that grant meaning to our lives. Perhaps this points to a new sense of responsibility that drives this book—the responsibility to inhabit such gaps, to dwell in the possibility of the unimagined: methodological responsibility as political practice. Herein lie productive considerations for risk and responsibility.

Lastly, I remain quite interested in discussions regarding the intersecting nature of inquiry, truth, truth-telling, and responsibility. In our contemporary moment it seems to have become the norm to discuss the first and last issues (inquiry and responsibility, respectively) without due consideration of the second and third (truth and truth-telling). As I note later in this book, this seems to extend from a simplified misreading of postmodern and poststructural theory, as though such theoretical orientations preclude overt assertions of truth. Further still, if questions of truth do arise, scholars of methodology or inquiry rarely articulate their own truth claims; that is, such scholars and theoreticians remain strikingly silent when it comes to their own beliefs or assertions of truth. This strikes me as decidedly limiting, as it situates the methodologist as nearly apolitical. In response, I advocate throughout this book for a different type of methodological engage-ment—one that extends from a specific form of truth-telling and remains overtly political—hence my development of methodological truth-telling, or *parrhesia*.

Simply put, *parrhesia* invokes a dedication to truth-telling, one that brings with it particular goals, contexts, and orientations toward knowing and living. To be specific, I define *parrhesia* throughout this book as *truth-telling with the aim of intervening within normative practices of knowing and being*. Such political interven-tions begin with a dedication to activate progressive change in the name of social justice. As I detail more specifically in Chapter 4, *parrhesiastic* activity can only occur when an individual risks his/her very citizenship within society. Thus, the truth-teller is necessarily caught up within the very interventions s/he invokes; the *parrhesiast* is never outside or otherwise removed from the social changes deemed necessary. In this way the term *parrhesia* evokes both an act (the truth-telling itself) and a relational-materialist orientation toward the world (that one can never tell the truth in isolation). Truth-telling as *parrhesia* thus exists at the intersection of methodological practice and philosophical beliefs of knowing and being. When we embrace *parrhesia*, we simultaneously embrace a relational engagement within the world. This, I think, is an important shift for methodologists who seek productive social change and is the motivation that caused me to write this book.

On Risk and Responsibility

Recently, at the American Educational Studies Association annual meeting, I benefited from an odd interaction with my panel's discussant. Following our panel, the discussant paused to ask me why I was so interested in risk and methodology: "I just feel like each new generation feels like it's the most cutting edge, doing the most cool and risky research out there," he said. "In the end, why don't you forget about risk and just do research? There's nothing wrong with being traditional, you know, when it comes to research." I asked him whether he had read my paper, he said he gave it a quick read, I complimented him on his shoes, and he walked out into the bustling hallway in search of the free coffee and odd muffin. I say I benefited from this interaction because it made me realize that my point had been missed—either he missed the point of my argument in his quick read of my paper or I failed to adequately articulate my notion of risk and inquiry in my talk or, of course, both.

Less recently I gave a talk at the University of Texas at Arlington on methodological responsibility, critical inquiry, and materialist methodologies. During the question-and-answer following my presentation a more senior faculty member raised his hand and commented, "When you talk about being responsible and ethical, you are talking about the IRB [institutional review board] process, right?" I laughed at his joke that, it turns out, wasn't a joke at all. And again I realized that my point had failed to reach its mark.

So I want to be clear from the beginning that I am decidedly *not* interested in conflating notions of *risk* with being *cutting edge* or *cool* methodologically. I've never been cool. Such is life. And I am not interested in situating my considerations of methodological responsibility within the technical discourse of procedurized ethics that is the Institutional Review Board. I will happily let others allow the dance of the IRB to stand in for their own ethical deliberations.[5]

Instead, I want to consider both *risk* and *responsibility* in relation to the logic that informs their historical definition within qualitative inquiry *and* I want to consider possibilities for thinking differently about these terms given our contemporary times of hyper-neoliberalism and globalization. In some ways, I suppose, I hope to situate these terms in a historically aligned context, one that problematizes both their (un)spoken definition and the logics that make them possible. To do so, I think, I need to begin from more macro-orientations and work through the rationalities and anxieties that make these terms possible.

Critical of Critical

There is an odd trend in educational scholarship that extends from a good degree of anxious energy regarding the terms *critical* and *critique*. The former seems particularly concerning for scholars in that nearly everyone wants to assign the term to their work, particularly within the auspices of methodology—everyone wants to be *critical*—and there is thus an erasure of the term from the method-ological literature. By erasure, I mean that the term has lost its meaning; indeed, the *word* critical seems everywhere these days, endlessly invoked within a host of fields and studies. As a consequence, *critical* seems to have been relieved of its generative meaning. It has simultaneously become both everything and nothing. There are a host of critical methodologies, critical forms of analyses, even (apparently) critical considerations of quantitative methodologies.[6] For me, *critical*—in relation to methodology—means something rather specific. It involves intervention. Further, I might submit that such interventions neces-sarily extend beyond the level of method. More than the techniques through which we generate data and (via analyses) make meaning, I remain most in-terested in those rationalities that make such methods visible, that afford them their raison d'être. This begins, I believe, through a shift in considerations of power—how it manifests and what it makes possible. As such, when I invoke the term *critical* throughout this book, I draw from Kincheloe and McLaren's (2005) notion of the criticalist.

In their overview of critical work within the field of education, Kincheloe and McLaren (2005) emphasize the confrontational elements of such practices: "'critical' must be connected to an attempt to confront the injustice of a par-ticular society or public sphere within the society" (305). This confrontational engagement must be ongoing and focused on the inconsistent discursive social patternings and material practices that are the inevitable result of social institu-tions, such as education. Unjust social structures are never static but manifest through their incessant reproduction within daily practices of meaning-making and relation. Critical engagement thus becomes emancipatory action through exposing the inherent contradictions and gaps in contemporary social forma-tions (Kuntz 2011b). Revealing seemingly fixed social structures as fluid and fraught with inconsistencies makes their easy reproduction less natural or assured. The criticalist, then, embodies a strategic turn away from static rep-resentations of our social world and toward a recognition of and engagement within an overlapping array of social processes—systems that often contradict and confront one another even as they remain hidden through the overarching norms of the common sensical or the status quo (Kuntz 2011b). This is critical work done in the name of social justice.

A similar sense of critical intervention might be found in the social justice framework that guides critical geography, as seen in the work of David Harvey. For Harvey (2001), critical scholarship disrupts the seemingly logical bifurcation between *facts* (the legitimate outcome of empiricism) and *values* (the ideologi-cally infused realm of humanism): "critical scholarship exposes the artificiality of the separation between fact and value and shows that the claim of science to be ideology-free is itself an ideological claim" (36). Thus, the critical scholar has two interwoven tasks: (1) to understand the means by which otherwise common-sensical rationales develop, producing a host of legitimated practices; and (2) to imagine or enable new practices that extend from newly possible forms of knowing. Harvey writes,

> In order to change the world, we have first to understand it. In order to change the world, we have to create new human practices with respect to the realities around us. . . . It is, of course, the task of critical and reflective thought to understand our condition and to reveal the potentiality for the future imminent in the present. (36–37)

Harvey's insights echo the necessary collapse of the past with the future in the present, discussed earlier as an important practice of methodological responsibility. As a critical scholar hailing from the Marxist tradition, Harvey sees "the task of critical and reflective thought" as activated through exposing the inherent contradictions within ideological formations as well as our creative capacity to be other than we are. Of course, the practices that inform such critical work necessarily shift and change, buffered by the influence of social assertions regarding reality and truth. In Chapter 4 I offer a renewed analysis of the transformative possibilities of critical work to intervene in the production of power-laden truth given our contemporary moment of multiple, simultaneous truths. What happens, for example, when the distinction between truth and falsity blurs so much that such differentiation no longer easily holds? What possibilities, what consequences reveal themselves in such a circumstance?

In short, critical work encourages ethically laden creative alternatives to normative rationalities and normalizing practices, a critical insubordination to traditional ways of knowing and coming to know. Returning to critical methodologies for a moment, we might thus see how inquiry processes that merely describe contemporary ways of being are far from critical. As such, these descriptive approaches miss the distinctive ethical imperatives that extend from critical approaches to inquiry. As Kuhn (2008) notes, the practice of inquiry is inherently an ethical practice that simultaneously extends from and continues a host of assumptions concerning knowing and being. It is in this sense that I conclude this chapter with a short overview of the ethical considerations that guide this book.

I have been influenced by the work of J. K. Gibson-Graham (2003, 2014) on the important connection between knowing and being as well as engaged ethics—that through changing how we come to know, we can simultaneously change how we come to ethically be. From this perspective, our theories need to do more than simply describe the world as it is; they need to challenge it even as they point to possibilities beyond our current constructions. An outcome from this is an ethically laden challenge of refusal—resisting the easy action of (re)constructing the very world in which we seek to intervene through our theoretical formations. As DeMartino (2013) asserts, "Knowing, here, is generative and constitutive—never merely descriptive" (489). This presents an important ethical dimension for the critical inquirer: what we know, how we come to know, is never socially neutral, never absent the import of the ethical frame. As a consequence, the responsible methodologist must offer new ways of thinking and being in the world even as s/he seeks to inquire into the world in which we live. Equally as important, those who teach inquiry must responsibly offer critical investigations into both practices of coming to know and the very rationalities/logics that make such knowing possible. It remains methodologically irresponsible to simply recreate what already exists, reproducing the norms and normative systems that make our world visible. This is to recreate the normalizing processes of common sense. As DeMartino writes, "Scholars' choices matter ... because they alter [the] world in ways that either illuminate and enable or obscure and disable strategies of transformation" (489). The ethical inquirer, then, is an engaged scholar, one who refuses the seductive framing of negative difference, of distancing knowing from being, of who we are from how we become.

The related second term, *critique,* seems to invoke distinctly negative emotions due to its overuse as an adversarial term—as though critique necessarily takes away or removes something from that which it engages. Importantly, there involves a creative capacity in the inquiry process, the ability to transition critique of the past or present into future possibilities. Thus, to critique is more than to simply offer criticism; it is to make newly possible, to expose cracks and interstices that otherwise escape processes of meaning-making so that we might live differently. Unfortunately, this creative element of critique is often lost in the rush to offer criticism: "To focus on what is bad and wrong is too often confused with gritty realism, when in fact it is sheer pessimism" (Sharpe 2014, 38). On the contrary, I find critique as endlessly optimistic—that we might locate where dominant perspectives of the world fall short and thereby make available new, previously unarticulated practices of everyday life. In this way critique usefully brings to the fore resistive practices that otherwise might remain unacknowledged. I return to this notion of optimistic critique in the concluding chapter of this book.

As Leask (2011) notes, resistance from a Foucauldian framework is made common: "it is for all, by all, and everywhere. . . . Resistance is where we begin; it is foundational" (10). Given this multiplicity of resistances, critique plays a key role in activating resistive practices with new meanings, toward new possibilities of being and becoming: "*critique* is fundamental if these oppositional energies are to be rendered efficacious or meaningful" (Leask 2011, 11, original emphasis). To engage in critique is to make new meaning possible, to draw together a host of entangled resistances toward the promise of a future that has yet to be. I take up this Foucauldian conception of critique as a creative form of resistance in more detail in Chapter 4's discussion of *parrhesia*.

Methodological Activism

In many ways I first point to the problem of distancing—of removal of the researcher-self from political and material contexts—and it is one that methodologists have discussed for many years now (e.g., Geertz 2001; Marcus and Fischer 1999; Rosaldo 1993). And yet I think it is important to reconsider this distancing specifically as it relates to intersections of the inquirer, methodological assumptions, and material practices of inquiry; that is, I want to question the easy separation and categorization of these entities that inevitably make their way into our research textbooks. This question begins with the problem of extraction and the normatively implied interactions of the individual, the inquiry approach, and methodological practice as actions between, as opposed to within.[7] Throughout this book I understand such relationality as a constellation of meanings, one well worth continued interrogation and reconstruction. Indeed, new constellatory formations perhaps make space for reconsiderations of truth-telling, methodological risk, and responsibility.

Further, there is a tendency, it seems, in some methodological circles to conclude that we have adequately disrupted our distancing methodological stances, that the problem of extraction is old news. However, I ask for newly risky engagement with these well-worn questions, ones that foreground a material relationality and responsible truth-telling. In line with Foucault's analysis of *parrhesia*, this is materially situated political work. Thus, in relation to traditional educational methodologists' seeming endless quest for more and increasingly "efficient" distancing and categorizing techniques of data production and analysis, it remains important to recognize the material consequences of such activities.

In short, there seems to be an ongoing crisis in educational research about what it is, what it is for, and how its "proper" value might be arbitrated (Peim

2009). I seek here to address this crisis and offer a renewed perspective of what inquiry may be, what it might make possible, and how it might be understood by foregrounding issues of responsibility and truth-telling that center on notions of risk and (material) relationality.

Conclusion

It is the possibility for methodological work as enacting productive difference that is the ultimate driving force behind this book. As such, it remains important to consider how the above overview of particular orientations toward knowing and coming to know operationalize select key terms in particular ways. Indeed, notions of *risk, activism, ethics,* and *responsibility* take on particular shape and form given this approach to relational living and being as well as the globalized, neoliberal context in which we currently operate. Unfortunately, such terms often remain undefined—or, like the term *critical* discussed earlier, defined so broadly and within such varying contexts that they lack any real communicative value. Yet these terms play a key role in my own analyses, and consequently, it would seem to make good sense to end this chapter with an overview of how I intend to utilize them in my arguments that follow.

Within our contemporary contexts the notion of *activism* takes on multiple definitions, some more useful than others. In a general sense, to engage in activism is to in some way work for social change. As such, activism requires an imaginative or creative element—the ability to understand ourselves as other than we are. More specifically, activism involves a determined intervention into the normative processes and practices that govern the world in which we live. As a practice of intervention, activism necessarily remains grounded in the realm of the material; activist practices are material practices. Through activism one might seek to generate new meanings, new ways of considering and engaging within the world. Unfortunately, contemporary manifestations of globalization and neoliberalism have had their limiting effects on how one might understand and practice activism, particularly within the realm of inquiry. The collapse of geographical boundaries and unfettered flows of capital that extend from the processes of globalization, mixed with the hyper-individualism and surveillance characteristic of neoliberalism creates rather confounding times for the individual bent on promoting progressive social change. At times it would seem that our collective activist practices draw all too well from the globalized, neoliberal values they seek to critique or otherwise disrupt. Activism might be seen to be virtualized, for example, in less than productive ways as we commit to some element of "change" through clicking a *like* button on our desktops or through adding our electronic signatures to some online petition.[8] Of course, these virtual acts, as a form of activism, are not inherently negative, yet they become more disappointing when aligned with the individualizing and isolating tendencies of neoliberalism. Indeed, activism itself requires connection—the refusal to understand oneself outside of relation.

What, then, might methodological activism look like? To begin, engaging in methodological activism is to construct methodologies that themselves work for change; that is, the methodological activist refuses to believe in the neutrality of inquiry methods, procedures, and analyses. Methodologies are inherently partisan—they extend from political engagements with knowing and coming to know. As Denzin (2010) asserts, "the qualitative researcher is not an objective, politically neutral observer who stands outside and above the study of the social world. Rather, the researcher is historically and locally situated within the very processes being studied" (23). This situatedness imposes a necessary inclusion of the activist self within the practice of critique. As Davies (2010) notes, practices of engaged, activist inquiry necessitate that one struggles "against oneself, against the normative force of language and everyday practice. It is a continuous struggle" (58). Struggles for social justice necessarily imply that the activist is both the impetus for and simultaneous object of productive change.

As such, methodological activism requires a degree of risk. And by risk, I do not simply mean employing methodologies that might generate "bad" data. Instead, in the same vein as Denzin and Davies, I would like to consider methodological risk in light of a key element of *parrhesiastic* practice: as engaging in work that chances the very political relations that inform our identities. We must risk ourselves if we are to truly engage in activist work; we must generate new ways of becoming. Through participating in new ways of knowing we come to engage in new ways of being—the intrarelation of it all continues as methodological activists agitate for new material possibilities not currently encountered. Through critique, old centers can no longer hold. As the work of J. K. Gibson-Graham (2003, 2014) consistently makes clear, our ontological formations are produced discursively even though we often consider our ways of being as determining what we know and how we come to know; what we once assumed as unidirectional is, instead, dynamically multidirectional. This productive intersection between being and knowing—that ways of knowing can come to alter ways of being—produces newly ethical considerations. Thinking and writing thus become endlessly productive, making possible alternative formations of being in the world.

Following this logic, inquiry more easily takes on an activist stance—inquiry as intervention into the world in the name of social justice. This is the task I set for this book. Such notions of *methodological activism* and risk extend from a new sense of *engaged ethics.* We must devise new ethical engagements if we are to live differently.

Chapter 2

Logics of Extraction

Introduction

Let me begin this chapter with an example from my own work as an identified professor of qualitative research methods. Often I am asked to serve on dissertations as a methodologist, and my colleagues seem to expect that I will take ownership of the onerous Chapter 3—traditionally the methodology chapter—particularly during prospectus and proposal meetings (Chapter 3 is all too easily overlooked in final dissertation defenses in favor of an excited discussion of findings and their significance—traditionally Chapters 4 and 5, respectively). That is, in dissertation meetings when the discussion moves to Chapter 3, all eyes turn down the table and rest firmly upon me. The hope, I suppose, is that I will make easy (easier?) work of challenging contexts: how many interviews to conduct, with whom, and how to thematically code the imagined transcripts of the future. Chapter 3 is offered as my responsibility. There are times, of course, when for the benefit of the student I should point to more traditional modes of "doing method." And there are times when I would do well to be more challenging, to openly question my positioning as a technocratic methodologist, whose role, it seems, is to bring order to otherwise unruly lived experience through the magic of method. The decision to intervene and disrupt the order of method is one I do not take lightly, and I find it my responsibility to do so with an aim of resisting extraction, of refusing methodological work that results in closure.

Unruly lived experience through method

So how did this come to be? How did my expertise as a methodologist translate to a particular type of responsibility for a particular section of the dissertation? In some ways these perspectives seem to follow a belief in efficiency and conceptions of particularized expertise: "I am a methodologist, Chapter 3 is my purview; the other chapters are best served by the content experts on the committee." Such values derive in no small way from current contexts of neoliberalism and globalization, two aligned discourses that manifest in select daily practices as "just making sense."

Throughout this chapter I seek to set the stage for what I see as the contemporary sociopolitical context in which traditional methodologies operate as well as the rationalities that have historically informed current connotations of methodological identity, practice, and responsibility—key terms that play no small role in how I am perhaps claimed by Chapter 3 during dissertation meetings. Briefly stated, today's methodologist has gained legitimacy as a field specialist or technocrat, a socially approved role not unlike that of the middle manager in the business world. Such conceptualizations of methodological identity and work extend from our neoliberal and globalized times. As a consequence, traditional formations of methodological work simultaneously pull from and contribute to processes of neoliberalism and globalization. Thus, rethinking the role of inquiry and those who conduct inquiry is itself an intervention into those conservative principles that so dominate the world in which we live. This is critical work.

As a normative technology, traditional qualitative inquiry finds justification in appeals to common-sensical means of knowing and coming to know (e.g., the continued invocation of the traditional interview, an all-too-often logical yet unquestioned research method. I examine the interview more directly later in this chapter). Norming technologies employed without critical thought require only technicians to distribute them and keep them running efficiently. In terms of methodological work, this scenario has made possible the *methodological middle manager*—one who specializes in applying codified techniques to produce knowable findings, a particularly risk-free methodological engagement. As a means for interrogating such historical formations, I begin this chapter with a contextual overview of how discourses of neoliberalism and globalization inform methodological identity and practice with implications for how we frame methodological responsibility and risk. Through neoliberal discourses and processes of globalization the methodologist has slipped into the role of a technocrat—known for the efficient production and management of verifiable forms of data. After establishing this curious circumstance, I then pay particular attention to manifestations of what I term a *logic of extraction,* with roots in post/positivistic and modernist claims regarding knowing and being that, in turn, find legitimation in—and extend—globalized neoliberal values. I end with an examination of how relational thinking might counter such limiting extractions and open new possibilities for those materialist methodologies that are the focus of Chapter 3.

The Production of the Methodological Technocrat: This Is Bullshit

There is a striking conceptual overlap between manifestations of the methodological technocrat and what Frankfurt (2009) terms the "bullshitter." This overlap extends from a shared disregard for questions of truth. In his description of *bullshit*, Frankfurt notes that the bullshit "statement is grounded neither in a belief that it is true, nor, as a lie must be, in a belief that [it] is not true" (46). In this sense bullshit ignores truth or disregards truth as having any implication on the statement. Such disregard distinguishes bullshit from lying: "it is impossible for someone to lie unless he thinks he knows the truth. Producing bullshit requires no such conviction" (46). Thus, bullshit ignores the question of truth even as it lacks the means to take a stand in relation to the production of truth. Importantly, Frankfurt goes on to note that this disregard for questions of truth makes bullshit more dangerous than the act of lying. Contrary to bullshit, lying requires an acknowledgment of some truth and the subsequent choice to obstruct or mislead in relation to that truth. Bullshit, however, remains unconcerned regarding questions of truth. As a consequence, "bullshit is a greater enemy of the truth than lies are" (48). These circumstances, I fear, find a parallel in what we know of the methodological technocrat.

Regardless of how one feels about the production of truth (or truths), I want here to point out the striking similarities between the production of bullshit and the context-independent method that typifies normative or traditional methodological work. As noted in Chapter 1, I think it time methodologists re-engage with questions of truth, however tentative they may be. In the very least, our methodological work should be invested enough in social change so as to take a stand on the world as it is and the world as it might be. And, as critically engaged scholars, we methodologists should recognize the many ways in which our practices have a hand in re-inscribing the normative status quo. In this vein I also think it time we methodologists refuse the role of the technocrat, one whose expertise comes from the production, assertion, and enactment of timeless methods that happily stand on the sidelines during discussions of truth: "The data speak for themselves; I just make them visible." In this way, I

Data speaks for themselves

suppose, I ask that methodologists interested in social justice work refuse to engage in bullshit, refuse to remove themselves and their work from questions of truth. Far too often "method" is articulated in textbooks or communicated in graduate coursework absent questions regarding the production of truth—this is method as bullshit. Our contemporary times call for more. No longer can methodologists pretend the disinterested stance. Perhaps the first step toward productive engagement is to understand the context of our times.

Methodology in Times of Neoliberalism and Globalization

Much has been written on the neoliberal context and its impact on education, learning, and identity—to name just a few of the social processes alluded to in this chapter thus far. And yet neoliberalism has become an annoyingly ambiguous word in much scholarship extending from the social sciences and education alike. Thus, I want to take a moment here to comment upon three key and entangled issues: (1) neoliberalism as the governing rationality of our times, (2) globalization as a complementary process that reinforces and extends neoliberal values, and (3) the impact of the first two issues on methodological identity and practice. Through globalized neoliberalism we are offered a logic of extraction with significant consequences for the political possibilities of methodological risk and responsibility.

Though neoliberalism is linked to globalization, the two are not one and the same. I write this despite a confounding determination in contemporary scholarship to freely substitute one for the other, seemingly without much care at all. From a Foucauldian perspective, neoliberalism manifests historically as an extension of the rationality of the market into areas of life that had not previously been understood in primarily economic terms. Neoliberalism shifts how we conceive of the family, for example, even as it marks individuals according to a host of metrics such as credit scores, health records, or educational attainment.

For my purposes, neoliberalism manifests within globalization as a particular form of governmentality[1] that privileges (1) *hyper-individualism* (that individuals "stand on their own two feet" regardless of social standing or need); (2) *hyper-surveillance* (that individuals should always make themselves visible or known through quantifiable determinations of value); (3) *economic determinations of productivity* (an individual's social worth is determined by his/her contributions to the economic sphere); and (4) *competitive entrepreneurialism* (successful individuals are those who can exploit market conditions in order to advance their social standing). Though certainly other normalizing values contribute to and extend from neoliberalism, I foreground these four elements for the benefit of conceptual clarity. Further, it remains an important facet of neoliberalism that these four values (and more) are produced as social norms, ways of being, so that individuals might choose them freely—we freely invoke such neoliberal assumptions as an act of our own manufactured agency. In large part neoliberalism governs by asserting freedom as the act of choosing according to neoliberal norms. As a simplistic example, I can (freely) go into a shoe store and (freely) purchase any shoe I want (as long as it is on the shelf and I have the economic means to do so). More in line with the focus of this chapter, I can (freely) choose any methodology and (freely) implement its technologies (as long as it produces recognizable data that can stand on their own explanatory power). Freedom as an act of neoliberal definition.

Following Foucault (2008), I understand neoliberalism as more than a historical context—it exists as a political rationality with its own assumptions about the way in which we understand and operate within the world. As a means for making sense, neoliberalism makes visible select ways of knowing and being even as it occludes others. As such, neoliberalism extends from a series of onto-epistemological assumptions. As Olssen and Peters (2005) note, neoliberalism as a political rationality is a "worked out discourse containing theories and ideas that emerge in response to concrete problems within a determined historical period" (315). Consequently, neoliberalism consists of making select problems recognizable even as it posits select responses to such problems as common-sensical. Conveniently, within a neoliberal framework problems and solutions are dynamically linked through those four normalized values described above.

Within the field of methodology, for example, we might recognize the "problem of voice" as a particular neoliberal concern with individualizing subjects through the commodification of "their" experience, a highly rational response to the question of historical silencing. Thus, there exist a host of methodological strategies invoked to claim voice where once there had thought to be silence (the lack of voice). Of course, there is nothing inherently wrong with wanting to resist a legacy of pushing oppressed people's experiences to the margins: often the specter of voice is invoked as part of a methodological procedure for locating/isolating/promoting voice in the name of social justice. The point is rather how these desires to locate particularized voice become transformed through neoliberal rationality in rather dangerous ways (I investigate this notion of voice a bit later in this chapter). We would thus do well to consider, even briefly, the impact of neoliberal rationality on higher education generally and the production of the methodologist more specifically.

Managing Education

A distinct outgrowth of neoliberalism within higher education has been an abrupt shift from values of *professionalism* (that privilege a peer-based system of evaluation and advancement) to that of *managerialism* (with its concomitant values of compliance and accountability as determined by measurable outputs) (Olssen and Peters 2005), and the field of methodology has certainly not been immune to this shift. Indeed, this move toward managerialism manifests select methodological practices that extend from the four elements of neoliberalism noted earlier. Taking voice as an example, methodological managerialism keys in on the hyper-individualism inherent in singular voice, a timeless representation of the subject that is best understood apart from or against collective history. This is voice as distinguished from and independent of more relational contexts. Principles of hyper-surveillance encourage methodological means for making singular voice visible and accountable. This is the voice of the agentic singular—one who remains responsible for identifiable causes producing discernible effects. More than establishing the singular subject, methodologically induced surveillance casts the now-visible subject into a neoliberal value system always on the lookout for those disciplinary actions necessary for maintaining or extending capitalistic function. Such functions draw in no small part from links between voice and values of *economic productivity*. Recognized (and recognizable) voices are those that extend from "productive" individuals. Your practices of economic citizenry grant you your voice. Those voices attributed to economically unreliable subjects (the unemployed, infirm, disabled, aged, and/or otherwise marginalized subject) are presented as extraneous or otherwise novel. Lastly, assumptions of neoliberal *entrepreneurship* situate your voice as your commodity—something to be bought and sold on the (methodological) market. These overarching principles of methodological managerialism collude, drawing as they do from a normative rationality that promotes an individualized, static, and discernible voice that is held accountable to values of economic productivity and the promise of entrepreneurial claims to be bought and sold on the methodological market.

In a critique of the impact of neoliberalism on higher education, Giroux (2014) points to the ease with which colleges and universities have become motivated by "an appeal to rationality" with an overemphasis on meeting economic goals and preparing students to meet the technical demands of the workforce (38). Increasingly faculty have followed this trend and are "defined less as intellectuals than as technicians and grant writers" (39). As such, the faculty member as technical manager of information relies on neoliberal rationality to give sense to his/her daily practices. This, in turn, creates a field of consistently rational activities and normative functions, the critique of which risks one's professional identity. Frankfurt (2009) notes the inherent link between rationality and consistency: "the heart of rationality is to be consistent" (40). What, then, if we do away with consistency when it comes to our methodological analyses? Further, what happens if we recognize the messy and often inconsistent nature of social interaction? It seems all too easy to render others as "irrational" simply because their actions or articulated rationale seems inconsistent (particularly in relation to globalized neoliberal values).

More specific to contemporary political considerations of the state, Harvey (2001) notes the privileging of rationality and efficiency as the de facto ethics for the neoliberal state. As a consequence, elements such as education and research—social processes imbued with social meaning—have become commodified, only recognized when visibly informed by the principles of rational consistency that so concern Frankfurt and Giroux.

This emphasis on rational consistency leads Harvey (2001) to recognize a corresponding increase in faculty docility, a key component of being "good citizens" who "prostitute our discipline before 'national priorities' and 'the national interest.'... The only solace to be gained, apart from our survival, is that this mentality is on a clear collision course with our sense of moral obligation" (33). It is perhaps this "clear collision course" that makes a reconsideration of methodological responsibility so timely: when our moral sense for social justice can no longer tolerate the passive technocratic ideals of neoliberal faculty work, productive change might well occur.

Though perhaps most visible within the academy in institutional processes such as tenure and promotion (the quantification of publication numbers and *impact factors* of journals on curriculum vitae, for example, or the cumulative amount of external funding as emblematic of professorial "worth") as well as an increased reliance on adjunct and contract faculty to manage the curriculum, this shift to faculty managerialism has a pronounced impact on methodological work and identity. Increasingly, the methodologist has become one whose expertise arises from an ability to manage data, to develop those technologies that simultaneously produce and legitimate select and codified representations of reality. In this sense, the methodological middle manager might be seen as a development of neoliberalism even as his/her activities accelerate neoliberal values concerning meaning and meaning-making. Of course, such neoliberal rationalities are hardly confined to local contexts. As such, neoliberal rationality is extended through its collusion with principles of globalization.

As Ben Kisby (2014) argues, globalization refers to a continuous interdependency of individuals and larger social forces that necessitate social intervention to order the otherwise unpredictable outcomes of changing societal relations. This relation of local and global forces produces a host of collective anxieties in need of resolution. Within the realm of education, for example, one finds significant concern that students from the United States are falling behind peers from other nations in fields such as mathematics and science. In this sense globalization is an unyielding momentum that characterizes some regions as "keeping up" while others "fall behind." A host of policy efforts and administrative practices are thus invoked to push US students to keep apace the widening relation of globalization.

Key to Kisby's overview of globalization is that policy makers readily accept globalization as a reality to which they must respond. These responses manifest as a series of policies, subjectivities, and practices that, in their very actualization, accelerate processes of globalization. So it is that the very response to the assumed reality upholds globalization as real; the self-perpetuating cycle continues unabated. Certainly one can find evidence of this in methodological orientations within the field of education. In order to know where students stand within the global order, for example, one must first make them visible through a series of comparable data. The privileging of such data reinforces select methods even as it provokes the anxious comparisons of "us" to "them," resulting in the rational implementation of educational policies such as No Child Left Behind and the Race to the Top.

Globalization intersects with neoliberalism in that the relational formation of the former is advanced by the governing values of the latter. Neoliberal principles and rationalities inform, for example, the privileging of select markers of math and science by which US students are judged as "falling behind." Further, the emergent identity of the methodologist as middle manager plays a key role in producing and maintaining those technologies that make neoliberal values visible within the globalized order. In this way, though regional locales have certainly been compared to the larger contexts of the global, it is the infusion of neoliberal values and rationalities that mark contemporary processes of globalization in dangerous ways. One particularly troubling manifestation of globalized neoliberalism as governing rationality is the methodological expert.

Embodied and Emplaced Within the Neoliberal Order

In order to concretize the interplay of neoliberalism with globalization, I would like to pause a moment to consider their relational impact on the methodological issues of embodiment and emplacement. Primarily neoliberal rationalities, when set within assumed realities of globalization, emphasize a virtualized body contained by virtualized spaces. One emphatic result from this overlapping process seems to be the eradication of select boundaries through the reassertion of neoliberal values. This process extends from what Deleuze (1995) termed the creation of the "dividual"—we have become *known* (made visible, recognized, and assessed) by the data we are said to produce. The dividual is considered in relation to a larger norming population. As a result, my physical "health" is read in the same way as my economic "health." The former might be determined through markers such as blood pressure, cholesterol count, or body mass index. The latter manifests through the newly ubiquitous credit score, salary, or degree of debt. As a consequence, bodies become normalized against large sets of data, a process that results in what Baez (2014) terms the "society of the statistic." As Patton (2010) notes, neoliberal forms of governing emphasize the extraction of

> dividuals where these are not whole persons but a certain number of functional aspects, each one defined in relation to particular ends. The dividual is a bundle of aptitudes or capacities such as the financial means that ensure a capacity to repay a bank loan or the scholarly aptitudes that guarantee entry onto a given program of study. A multiplicity of dividuals do not constitute a mass of people but rather a sample or a data-bank that can be analysed and exploited for commercial, governmental or other ends. (96)

In short, the dividual might be seen as the conversion of people into segments of data. Once my body becomes converted to data (here interpreted according to the same neoliberal rationale and values that define my economic health), I lose the affective qualities of my embodiment. Although this is perhaps most easily recognized in more quantitative research, it appears in qualitative approaches as well. This is perhaps best evidenced by two historical occurrences: the privileging of linguistic data (and those methods and analyses that produce and consume such data respectively) and the establishment of material bodies and places as containers from which data are extracted.

As Cole (2011) asserts, "much of the earnest and well-meaning philosophy and research behind educational practice is made redundant when the economic stance is taken into account" (8). This is to say that economic concerns regarding workforce preparation and individual productivity crowd out more social concerns regarding issues, skills, and knowledges that are not directly aligned with market-based values. In this scenario the "earnest and well-meaning philosophy" that informs critical methodological practice is pushed to the side in the decided rush to align method with the production of recognizable forms of data, made visible through the extractivist claims of traditional analyses. As Davies (2010) notes, traditional readings of the fixed subject emphasize a restriction of individual agency within neoliberalism, one with a "reduced capacity to generate new thought" (54). This sense of reduced agency occurs simultaneously to the hyper-individualization that is part and parcel with neoliberal norms. Giroux (2014), in turn, points to the many ways in which principles of neoliberalism strip economic and political discourses of their alignment with the social—economic and political rationales are distinguished from the weight of social costs through their imagined positioning as objective and neutral ways of knowing and doing. The result, in Giroux's words, is "the flight of critical thought and social responsibility" from economic, political, and—I would add—educational institutions (37).

Given the manner by which neoliberal values foreground the production of dividuals, all the while maintaining a nostalgia for the unified subject, we might seek to better understand how traditional qualitative methodologies manage this apparent contradiction. Though perhaps initially interpreted as in opposition, these two formulations might be productively read as reconciled through the rendition of qualitative inquiry as a technology. In this sense the methods, techniques, and practices that form qualitative research allow for both discrete subjects and particularized elements of representational data to sit side-by-side in apparent harmony. As I will go on to show, traditional approaches to qualitative research manage these contradictory values through invoking a *logic of extraction*—a rationale that foregrounds the separation of data (be they measures of health or representations of full subjects) from material context. This is qualitative research as a mediating technology. What remains consistent between these two presentations of data is the objective positioning of both the whole self (as always there, ready to be discovered, beyond direct influence from the immediate environment) *and* the self-as-segmented-data (the dividual as a *natural* product of meaningful markers, economically situated stand-ins for identity and worth).

Like representations of bodies as virtual data, principles of globalization virtualize space, erasing geographical boundaries through methodological practice. In particular, Rice and Vastola (2011) point to the impact of neoliberal rationalities on conceptions of who we are, how we come to know, and assumptions regarding being—identity, epistemology, and ontology, respectively. The authors note that the neoliberal epistemology "often links the rhetoric of choice to the reality of economic insecurity and the disruption of identity" (154). This link between choice, insecurity, and identity produces particular manifestations of a "risk society" wherein the dismantling of social support systems is (re) presented as an "opportunity" for (directed) choices for economic engagement and definition. This, in turn, encourages particular articulations of a globalized "common sense"—actions, identities, and values drawing from the economic realm for definition. Importantly, such normalized neoliberal ways of knowing and being are enhanced by ever-new technologies that, in turn, reinforce normative epistemologies and ontologies: neoliberal rationalities make possible particular technologies that are driven by—and drive—neoliberal rationalities. The serpent swallows its tail. For Rice and Vastola, this circulatory process finds meaningful traction through the production and use of segmented data— "particular signifiers" that "disregard context" and circulate "the same, tired methodologies" (155). What such a process needs, then, is someone skilled at manipulating those technologies that manifest and interpret such data for consumption. Enter the educated (read: disciplined) methodologist.

There remains an uneasy alignment between contemporary manifestations of research (within the neoliberal era) as technocratic practice and the production of the modern state as governing a *population* (themselves in need of normalizing technologies for control). As Foucault (2008) points out, the modern state employs select techniques that draw their meaning from considerations of population—the management of large groups of people within a select territory. With the advent of population, things like birth and infant mortality rates, credit scores, and literacy rates provide a governing rationale for imposed regulations, often employed with the aim of increasing the "health" of the population according to some confected norm. Education is thus employed to reinforce select norms, to produce a degree of self-regulation.[2] Within such a configuration the technocrat reigns supreme, offering order and (normalizing) coherence to the information produced by a population. Thus it is that the educational researcher has come to play such a normalizing role within this system—rarely risking his/her role as a researcher with the skills and abilities to interpret and disseminate information. This is the educational researcher as bureaucrat, "concerned with the order of society, the well-being of the population and the training of citizens. . . . The bureaucrat is someone who detaches him/herself from ethical and personal … commitments in order to be able to be involved in the administration of the population (as "objective", "neutral", "impersonal", "detached")" (Simons, Masschelein, and Quaghebeur 2005, 821). This bureaucratic emphasis on detachment aligns well with the globalized neoliberal values that sustain *logics of extraction.* Methodological bureaucracy relies upon research technicians for continued advancement. This is a detachment from inquiry processes and the moral values that inform them. As others have noted (see Hunter 1994; Simons, Masschelein, and Quaghebeur 2005) the researcher necessarily engages in pedagogical activities as well—training future researchers in practices of extraction and the province of reason over meaning-making. More than apathetic resignation that such socialized values and practices will forever be reproduced, we need morally engaged stances on inquiry that operate on premises of necessary change. This perhaps extends from critical engagement with conceptions of methodological expertise.

Neoliberal Claims on Expertise

Importantly, an extension of the rationality that governs—and makes governable—our lives is the production of the expert, and this specific element would seem to have rather vast implications for educational theory and practice. Much has been made, for example, about the formation and role of the research expert—one whose identity is in no small part manufactured through the collusion of a series of reified practices and technologies. And much anxiety has been shown about whether one can claim the title of methodologist and what such a marker means within educational discourse. These claims often assume particular renderings of what it means to be methodologically risky and responsible within our contemporary times. In some ways my discussion of contemporary manifestations of the educational expert overlaps with Michael Apple's (2005) conception of *new managerialism,* a contributing element to his notion of *conservative modernization.*[3] For Apple, the new manager provides the technical assistance to enact and manage policies of conservative modernization. The new manager is the technocrat, an expert in the facilitation of those technologies that elaborate and maintain neoliberal structures. Here lies a fixation on the procedures of coming to know—the incessant production of prescribed methodological techniques aimed at producing extracted forms of data, rendered meaningful through detached mechanisms of analysis. For the methodological middle manager, considerations of risk and responsibility seem disappointingly focused on risky techniques and technologies of inquiry. This, I believe, was the line of thought invoked by my discussant friend (referenced in Chapter 1) who dismissed risk as a simplistic attempt to make traditional methods hip and cutting edge—the latest trend walking the methodological catwalk with daring grace. If this were indeed the case, then I think I would agree with him: "No, there really is nothing wrong with engaging with traditional methods of inquiry." But this misses the deeper issues at hand here: we need to question the very rationalities and logic systems that grant traditional approaches their normative visibility, their consistent deployment as a matter of course and without the risk of critical engagement. Perhaps we could be more critically responsible, more disruptive than acquiescent, through extending different claims on considerations for *expertise.*

Disruptive Methodological Possibilities

Critics of neoliberalism from a critical geography perspective point to the easy annihilation of distance, local boundaries, and histories in the interest of more generalized (and generalizable) values that eradicate local borders through attempts to forage connections within a globalized market. In this way the local becomes subsumed by the global and its corresponding neoliberal rationalities: "the local is only defined as local through the very global epistemology to which it stands in contradistinction" (Rice and Vastola 2011, 156). This results in the "over saturation of the local by the global" (159), foregoing micro- or immediate histories, traditions, and values in favor of more universalizing values that (at best) obscure or (at worst) erase more regional formations of difference. Though traditional methodologies might be shown to extend such erasure through serving as a technological means for fixing meaning-making in particularly neoliberal ways, there also lies the possibility for our inquiry practices to productively disrupt such normative practices.

Rice and Vastola (2011) note the consequences of contemporary intersections among technologies of knowing, contexts of neoliberalism and globalization, and particular manifestations of agency and identity: "we already inhabit a moment where notions of identity, agency, and free choice, in their connection with new technologies, consistently fail to describe a substantive diversity at odds with a global, consumptive-driven economic imperative" (149). In this sense our contemporary contexts collude with technologies to produce particular formations of agency and identity that draw their definition from "a global, consumptive-driven economic imperative" (derived, of course, from principles of globalization and neoliberalism). In the face of this, Rice and Vastola interpret this contemporary moment as one of possibility for "real change" (149)—namely new identities, actions, and ways of coming to know that exist outside the normatively defining contexts of neoliberalism. In my better moments I share their optimism; indeed, if "real change" is to occur, it may be possible because new epistemological and ontological assumptions are warranted, even necessary. This possibility extends from the hyper-pessimistic activism that I share with Foucault's critical orientation within the world.

This brief overview of the complementary relation of globalization and neoliberalism is meant as background to the *logic of extraction* that dominates methodological thinking in our current age. Indeed, as the next section shows, the *logic of extraction* extends neoliberal values and situates methodological work as appropriate for our globalized times. The *logic of extraction* is part-and-parcel with the political rationality that is neoliberalism. This extension is perhaps most visible in formations of methodological responsibility and risk, with very real ramifications for how we understand inquiry in the name of social justice.

Logics of Extraction and Social Justice Work

Generally stated, what I term the *logics of extraction* refers to a conservative system of rationality that privileges discrete, fully knowable entities that remain consistent across time and space, absent the immediacy of material context. This logic both draws from and informs neoliberal values within an assumed context of globalization. I emphasize the term *extraction* because this logical system (what some, following Foucault, might term a methodological regime of truth) assumes that the most efficient and productive means for accessing knowledge is to make something "knowable" through extracting it from the immediate context in which it manifests. Thus, the "best" methods are those that expedite the extractive process. In this way *logics of extraction* serve and enable the neoliberal project—subjects become known through their very extraction; once extracted, they may be rendered in starker definition and made to relate to other extracted subjects.

Logics of extraction thus offer unique methodological consequences and might be understood as productive in particular ways. From the outset, extractive logics require that relations and processes assume a fixed state, cut off as they are from the emergent contexts of the immediate. Thus, those methods that attend to *logics of extraction* excel at producing *things,* objects for analysis. Such objects—and the legitimated methodological techniques that have a hand in their definition—offer the illusion of full or complete knowledge; that some *thing* could (and should) be fully known. This surety offers a confidence in (extracted) findings that is seductive to students and seasoned researchers alike. It offers ordered knowledge, the illusion that one can come to sense through pulling out or extracting the thing one wishes to examine. As one may imagine, a host of methodological practices have historically been invoked in attendance to the *logic of extraction.* These are the techniques that compel otherwise messy meanings toward order and are most often championed in methodological textbooks that offer a "cook's tour" of methodological approaches. Though such texts might offer distinctive chapters on, say, phenomenology, grounded theory, or case study, they are united by their allegiance to and advocation of *logics of extraction.*[4]

Of course, even while extractive logic makes possible select ways of being, knowing, and coming to know, adherence to such a perspective also forecloses other ontological, epistemological, and methodological practices. Perhaps foremost, *logics of extraction* presume fixity and stasis of the object of study, thereby rendering impossible relational approaches to being and knowing; there simply is no means to attend to unbounded processes or relations of which the inquirer is a part (the inclusion of the inquirer in the phenomena of study is often negatively referenced as bias and in need of strict methodological discipline). This extractive logic can only operate from a distanced perspective, where the inquirer stands decidedly outside that which s/he inquirers *into.* This has rather stark implications for critical methodologists intent on promoting some element of social justice: social change can only happen *out there,* distanced from the immediate contexts in which the inquirer is him/herself immersed and known. In this instance, social change is necessarily procedurized.

As a categorizing mechanism, the *logic of extraction* remains a driving force behind the procedurization of inquiry, lending validity to extractive methods and historical legitimacy to the rationalities that support them. Further, this *logic of extraction* must necessarily be understood as an outgrowth of neoliberalism— a continued political rationality with particular values and assumptions that, in turn, inform the daily practices of methodological work. What, then, does such extraction look like, and what are its effects?

Extractive Circumstance

In a general sense the *Oxford English Dictionary* defines the verb "extract" as "to draw out" or "to take from something of which the thing was a part." Later definitions of the term point to the force of this removal: "to get out ... by force, effort" and "to draw forth ... against a person's will" ("extract"). I cite these definitions because processes of extraction have become all too familiar in inquiry processes—the extraction of "data" for analysis, for example, has nearly become common-sensical and engaged without pause. In my own work with students and methodological conversations with colleagues I am often struck by the ease with which extractive procedures of meaning-making are given without consequence, naturally occurring facts of meaning-making without the violent force of removal implied by those secondary definitions of the term.

Consider for a moment the standard interview (a primary technology for the production of voice, noted earlier) wherein a participant's meaning-making is reduced to a voice in a data file that, in turn, is processed into a transcript (the actual event of the interview has thus moved from a materially situated interactive telling [the interview] to disembodied voice [the recording], to text [the transcript]), which is then categorized by a series of codes, which may or may not be considered in relation to one another (now textual representation—of voice, of experience—shifts to purely metaphorical articulation), which is then situated within some evidence-revealing text (the paper, manuscript, or dissertation). Such inquiry procedures force meaning-making into strict disembodied metaphorical relations—sounds, texts, words, and narratives *stand in* for materially situated experiences (this, of course, is the very nature of metaphor—it stands in for something rather than being the thing-in-itself). Consider also the required contextual shift that goes hand-in-hand with this commonsensical practice: by the time the written text is produced, we have lost the material context of the interview in favor of purely text-based relations (codes find meaning in relation to other codes, metaphors in relation to other metaphors). In many ways context becomes decontextualized. Further, this technical process is driven through the creation of select products: the interview recording, the transcript, the codes, the written report. Together such products signify progress—the steady movement toward finalized meaning. Individually such items stand ready as evidence of "proper" meaning-making (they represent legitimate markers for validity).[5]

Of course, this seemingly easy movement among self, voice, text, and product is not without consequence—such methodological steps should be troubled to reveal the logic that informs them. Importantly, we cannot forget the force of such removal or determined metaphorical relation—extracting data should never be an easy thing, engaged without political consequence. There is a violence to extraction that traditionally goes unnoticed in the procedurization of the inquiry process. In our fixation on method we perhaps miss the underlying assumptions that make such extractions possible. And I am not convinced that this process, codified and organizationally pleasing though it may be, is the best way to go about meaning-making. There are consequences for such efficiency. As such, it may be helpful to look more intently at the problem of the interview—what it makes possible, how it is known, and what might be missed in its traditional enactment.

Making Sense of Being: The Problem of the Interview

In order to consider the interview as an oddly commonsensical approach to meaning-making, I begin with an anecdote, cited by Certeau, regarding the conflict of being and interpretation: "When someone asked him about the meaning of a sonata, it is said, Beethoven merely played it over" (2011, 80). Often in qualitative inquiry it seems that we ask people for the meanings behind actions or the interpretation of particular events, at the risk of losing sight of the material-ness of the happening itself. In short, there should seem something odd about making an object of analysis out of our daily practices of living or meaning-making. And yet, of course, there is a veritable cottage industry of how-to books concerning qualitative research—containing a vast array of codified techniques and procedures for extracting meaning from observations, for example, or interview transcripts. Such procedures all aim to better define and more efficiently or effectively produce our experiences as objects to be known. Perhaps the most ubiquitous form of research practice in texts such as these is the interview. Whether standardized or open-ended in form, the interview is consistently offered as a more or less direct mechanism for generating representations of experiences, linguistically centered formations of data that are ripe for interpretation. This fixation on interpretation, it seems to me, has particular consequences that often remain absent in discussions of method. In particular, this formulaic approach to inquiry overlooks the material imprint of our modes of being even as it seeks to contain the dynamic contours of living. More simply stated, the move toward analysis most often is accompanied by what should be an uncomfortable claim regarding the need to extract—*that we cannot know anything that is not or cannot be contained unto itself, absent the material flow of relation.*

And so I wonder about the many ways in which our practices in qualitative inquiry ask others for their interpretation, their making sense of the story over and above the experience of being itself. This seems especially telling in the overemphasis in qualitative research on the interview as a mechanism for understanding experience and processes of meaning-making.

Part of the extractive simplification involved in the traditional interview is its swift and easy movement toward representationalism in the name of meaning-making. Representationalism derives from a Cartesian view of the world, an emphasis on inside and outside, with knowing subjects (insiders who experience) and more objective observers (outsiders who interpret). This belief in the authenticity of insider experience, represented by a shared external language, is a pervasive cultural assumption, promoted by an individualizing, consumerist society and sustained by logics of extraction. In this way the traditional interview utilizes and extends the values of our globalized neoliberal context. Indeed, McLaren's (1995) articulation of the American "predatory culture" is instructive here:

> In our hyper-fragmented and predatory postmodern culture, democracy is secured through the power to control consciousness and semioticize and discipline bodies

by mapping and manipulating sounds, images, and information and forcing identity to take refuge in the forms of subjectivity increasingly experienced as isolated and separate from larger social contexts. (117)

Here McLaren points to the intersection of neoliberal culture with those techniques of interpretive manipulation that sustain a felt sense of isolation and alienation. Through "mapping" the experiences of others in a way that separates knowing from being, traditional forms of the interview contribute to the "hyper-fragmented and predatory" status quo that is detrimental to social justice projects seeking social change. A critical analysis of the traditional interview reveals the many ways in which method both reflects and extends such normative processes.

When I teach my graduate classes in qualitative inquiry, I am often struck by the intense desire—on behalf of students and their advisers alike—to know the "proper" way to "do interviews"; that is, there remains a strong focus on procedural actions of writing interview protocols, asking questions, recording responses, producing transcripts and codes, and communicating findings. In many ways this is a disciplining of the interview—forming a method through the invocation of select constraints and prescribed procedures. And, of course, there is a doubleness to the discipline: both the prescribed method and the researcher encounter disciplining effects (similarly, in the research classroom both teacher and student respond to such discipline, both are subjected to the interview method they discuss). To invoke McLaren's language, the traditional interview represents a hyper-fragmented, manipulated version of reality, one that isolates and separates materially situated experiences from the very contexts in which they emerge. Indeed, the very process of *producing* the interview—of making it visible to and known by the researcher—confines it to the status of a *thing*, a commodity packaged for the interpretive market. There are multiple levels of loss here as the interview is produced—material circumstances of connection, for example, drop away in the audio recording of the interview, even as the physical markers of living (the extended breath, the thoughtful smack of enunciation) drop away in the transition to the transcript. In short, the traditional interview might be read in Marxist terms as procedural reification: the production of a *thing*—in this case, *the* interview—out of materially situated relations. Whose interests are served by the production of methodological things, interviews rendered as commodities or otherwise reified procedures?

In such a scenario the methodologist derives recognizable expertise from making light work of such reification—of making visible interview-objects that can bear the weight of interpretation and hold up as markers of meaning.

Of course, such extractive processes, here manifesting in the production of the interview, intersect with more macro-orientated sociopolitical trends and contexts (hence the link of interview practices and consequences with larger-ordered manifestations of neoliberalism). Such circumstances highlight the need to reconsider our responsibility to methodological practice.

This patterned thingification of the interview, while making possible a host of extracted possibilities, is not without consequence. What remains troubling is that the repeated invocation of this procedure has resulted in systematic extraction as legitimized proper ways to "do interviews" (and the inevitable expressed frustration and rolled eyes students toss my way as I seek to productively disrupt such easy extraction). Indeed, I often remark that it is perhaps my job to make extraction more difficult, not ease the transition away from the material event that is the event of the interview.

Beyond the recognition of the traditional interview as entangled with ongoing processes of reification, I take the normative use of the interview as caught up in what Foucault (2010) terms *technologies of power*, those entities aimed at producing knowledge about both the population and the individual. By abstracting the body and the material environment and, instead, emphasizing overly linguistic interpretations of meaning, inquirers are offered a narrow and simplistic array of choices for interpretive action. This narrowing of possibility remains a key component of governmentality, a process of governing that seeks to limit possible actions and thus increase the ease of government or control. Governmentality generates "actions upon actions," foregoing the strict control of bodies (as seen in Foucault's notion of *discipline* and alluded to in my earlier analysis of the interview as disciplining both method and methodologist) in favor of setting limits on perceptions of what can be known and what activities are even possible within particular contexts. Governmentality emphasizes alterations to the "rules of the game" as a mechanism for achieving select goals or ends (thus governmentality does not act directly on bodies themselves—changing the rules invites us all to alter our practices accordingly). In this way the object of knowledge is not material bodies or environments but *activities* and the production of rationalities that grant them their meaning. Therefore, it simply *makes sense* that students and their advisers fixate on the correct rules for conducting interviews; the rules invoke a governing force. Method thus becomes a governing technology, with the methodologist as one who facilitates that process. The result is a social docility that re-invokes normative ways of knowing and coming to know. Through the traditional interview, inquirers, no matter how well intentioned, return to a Cartesian duality that extracts the body and material world from processes of meaning-making. Absent body and material contexts, we are subjects once more, not easily participants in the production of our own meaning. Such effects extend out of the traditional interview not just as method but as a technique situated within a particular contemporary context. In this sense we should properly return to the scorned term "research subjects": we *subject* others to the interview even as we subject ourselves to the logics invested in interview technologies. We are all *research subjects*; simply asserting the euphemistic terminology of "research participants" does little to alter such circumstance.

As Brinkmann (2011) notes, the "modern consumer society is an interview society" (57). Brinkmann goes on to assert that the interview enjoys such legitimacy and privilege due to its "softer seductive forms of power through dialogue, narrative, empathy, and intimacy" (57). The interview, then, holds a doubly seductive sway in our contemporary world: existing as a technology aimed at seducing truths from participants—a method aimed at the inner narratives of their lives—even as it seduces the inquirer to take up its cause in the name of the whole or unified humanist subject. As a reified *thing,* the interview activates a host of cultural norms and values that legitimize and privilege particularly contained selves encountering external experiences resulting in "unique" individual insights (your experiences are yours alone—your narrative is unique—and through the magic of method I can both honor its uniqueness *and* connect it to larger cultural experiences and/or a select group of themes and theories found in the literature). In this sense both the interviewer and interviewee are caught up in the dance of humanism, each adhering to conceptions of the interview as a "central technology of the self ... where nothing is or must remain hidden, and where selves are commodified conversational products" (Brinkmann 2011, 57). The enclosed, containable self is created through the interview technology so that it might then be consumed. The humanist dance thus has shown itself to be cannibalistic in nature.

Additionally the traditional interview process maintains a mystification of the body that, in turn, allows for a distancing of the researcher, a (mis)recognition that researcher and participant bodies no longer matter. Thus, the use of the interview in qualitative research, for example, extracts language-as-data from the material and embodied contexts in which such utterances were spoken and of which they are expressions. This leads Brinkmann (2011) to assert that "too many interviews today are conducted based on ... a spectator's stance—a voyeur's epistemology or an epistemology of the eye" (59). The privilege of the researcher to remain an extracted, disembodied spectator reinscribes the very inequitable power formations in which critical qualitative inquiry seeks to intervene, seen namely in the production of the *humanist subject.* So how do we change such circumstances? How do we intervene in such methodological governing?

Elizabeth St. Pierre (1997) advocates for approaches to inquiry that shift away from the humanist subject to an emergent *poststructural subjectivity*. The distinction of a subject from subjectivity is important as it signals a transition away from logics of extraction to more relational means of identification. The humanist subject emphasizes an enclosed, static subject that, in turn, establishes a clear sense of internal and external (a division that separates the individual from the multiple contexts in which s/he is immersed). This is the subject the traditional interview seeks and interview methodologies produce. The static humanist subject demonstrates a strong sense of self-definition and determination: *I have a core self that can be known and remains unchanged across time and space.* Tracing the consequences of the humanist subject reveals privileged subjects that are rendered more legitimate over time. With each new invocation, the normative subject (re)asserts its privilege as that against which all subjects are known. Such subjects are often generalized in contemporary culture according to globalized neoliberal assumptions of value, defining, for example, what it means to be a productive citizen or recognizable person within a society—most often according to economic claims.

In contrast to the static and ahistorical humanist subject St. Pierre offers poststructural subjectivity, an ongoing process of formation that extends from multiple, often contradictory discourses with no uniquely centered essences or timeless truths. Thus, poststructural subjectivities alleviate concerns for locating "authentic" selves or developmental narratives of coming-to-oneself. Through advocating for the displacement of humanist subjects with poststructural subjectivities, St. Pierre (1997) offers an ethical imperative to alter the habitual systems of logic through which we traditionally confect meaning. In her words, we must "think differently than we have thought" (2). This is, of course, no easy task. If we take St. Pierre seriously, we must forgo the comfortable language of the humanist subject—no longer can we proclaim the assumed value of getting to the "core" or "truth" of a subject. We may no longer ask participants to narrate the assumed linear trajectory of their lived lives and employ techniques such as the traditional interview to make them more visible. In short, St. Pierre takes from us our humanistic "mother tongue" and sets us the task of "getting free" of ourselves (2). As St. Pierre notes, traditional methodologies, such as the standard interview, do little to disrupt the production of humanist subjects; indeed, they most often recreate them.

Within the context of the interview, displacing the humanist subject disrupts the normative subject positions that are privileged in our contemporary context.

Further, doing so makes space for new formations of knowing and being. Inquiry that displaces the humanist subject refuses a centralized, contained individual who may be known through prescribed methods and within extracted circumstances. Traditional interviews perhaps lose their governing power. In order to enact this shift toward poststructural subjectivities, we need alternative ways of knowing, being, and coming to know. We need to develop means of thinking and being not based on principles of extraction.

Responding to Extractivist Logic—Newly Responsible Practices

In order to productively respond to the extractive assumptions seen in the traditional interview, it is perhaps helpful to re-imagine how we come to know and those daily practices that inform our knowing. The work of Certeau (1984) proves helpful here, as he remains suspicious of method, of the way in which it asserts particular formations of *know-how*. For Certeau, method seeks to overturn and separate out what he terms "the relation between knowing and doing" (65). To use the language invoked in the chapter thus far, method extracts knowing from doing. In this sense method "sets off practices articulated by discourse from those that are not (yet) articulated by it"—it cuts off possibility in favor of ordered certainty (65). Here method has a particularly insidious sorting effect, causing some elements of being to be known or deemed knowable while others are dismissed, rendered outside traditional formations of knowledge. Given the incestuous relation of globalized neoliberalism, logics of extraction, and procedurized methods described earlier, Certeau perhaps provides an inroad to useful considerations for how such relations grant traditional inquiry social legitimacy, thereby establishing as valuable a select set of practices built on foreclosure.

Specific to my interest in this chapter, Certeau's sense of method is one of making known—truth-telling—through extracting and making "things" of daily practices. These are not, of course, apolitical acts. This causes Certeau (1984) to ask what happens to those practices, ways of being, that exist without discourse or, as he puts it more directly, "discourse without writing" (65).[6] What happens to those material practices not caught up in the conceptual net of the *logic of extraction*? What happens to those excesses that cannot be accounted for in traditional research paradigms? These are the practices of everyday life that are alluded to in the title of Certeau's most famous text and, I believe, offer a material context that is often denied in educational inquiry. Method thus offers "proper" analyses that turn words and actions into things, and such things, in turn, can stand in for living. The force of such circumstances is that research fixates on experiences-as-extracted-things; *experience* stands in as a proxy for everyday life. Think of the multiple ways in which we in the qualitative community have called upon experience to signify multiple elements of living or being. We ask participants to speak of their experiences in interviews, we translate others' experiences into new contexts, and so on. In this way we invoke the term *experience* to signify the methodological capture of the humanist subject.

This methodological fixation on experience causes Desjarlais (1997) to question its usefulness as an overarching representation of lived material reality. Through his critical ethnography of a homeless shelter for the mentally ill in Boston, Massachusetts, Desjarlais points to a cultural assumption that experience develops through an interiority that seamlessly links time and space into some discernible narrative of being. *This is* my *experience. Let me frame it for you. It begins* here *and ends* there. *At its core, is* me. In contrast, Desjarlais finds that the participants in his ethnography do not experience the world as traditionally rendered in qualitative inquiry; they lack the cohesive sense of self moving through time and space that seems a requirement of the term. Without experience, they are not recognized (or recognizable) subjects. Their lack of cohesive or narratable experience remains emblematic of their mental illness. By not claiming (or being claimed by) some unifying experience, they are forever removed from the interpretive lens of standardized methodologies. Their daily practices of living extend beyond the reach—in excess of—traditional research methods and the extractive logics that inform them. As a result, Desjarlais refuses to position the residents of the homeless shelter within the extracted realm of experience. And in doing so he finds that traditional methodological formations fail him. This presents a methodological quandary that I often ask students: What are we to do if the term *experience* is no longer available to our inquiry projects? What is lost—indeed, what is gained—if the term is removed from methodological circulation? Given this, what are we to make of this conceptual overlay of experience as extending from and indicative of humanist subjects? To paraphrase Derrida (1983): *How can we* not *think of experience?*

Though Desjarlais productively questions our reliance on experience, I worry that our traditional inquiry methods do not do enough to disrupt such an extractive and metaphorically reliant rationale. Indeed, most often, it seems, practiced inquiry re-affirms such extraction as normalizing experience, over-emphasizing linguistic renditions of experience, for example, over the material contexts of being or living.

Returning to Certeau's (1984) critique of method reveals our contemporary fixation on extraction and, consequently, that we only come to know that which may be *transported,* cut away from the circumstances of being. Certeau writes, "What cannot be uprooted remains by definition outside the field of research" (20). In this sense research practices aim to both uproot (or extract) partial meanings and then delegitimize all else as excessive or outside the scope of the inquiry project. Qualitative researchers are thus left with what Certeau terms "movable elements." Such movable elements remain all too often the object of our inquiry, distanced and detached from the very material contexts from which they have been transported. Perhaps more importantly, the production of extracted objects for analysis requires little risk, or the risks themselves remain at the level of the procedural. Perhaps we have a responsibility to think, act, and be in other ways. In order to do this, we may need to differently orient to those phenomena we deem worthy of our critical inquiry.

In line with Certeau's "moveable elements," made possible by the methodological procedurization of extraction, is his differentiation of *knowledge from above* and *knowledge from below,* resulting in *strategic* and *tactical* formations of knowledge respectively. Knowledge from above provides maps and "tour knowledge"—that is, static, contained, ordered space and prescribed, manufactured knowledge of such maps. This, according to Certeau, gives the researcher access only to strategic formations of knowledge: subjects extracted from local contexts and, instead, understood solely against larger social institutions. In a way knowledge from above offers the map of experience that Desjarlais seeks to resist. Traditional inquiry methods, such as the standardized interview, make the map orderly and sensible. As Kenway and Hickey-Moody (2011) articulate, "the map and the tour regulate knowledge and power. . . . Tour knowledge is 'how to' knowledge; it steers people along predetermined routes and shows them how to behave along the way" (153). Specific to our methodological work, it seems we are all too concerned with the production of ordered maps and procedurized knowledge as a means to make manifest our inquiry. Methodological procedures map out experience, confining ways of being and knowing to the logical progression the term entails. This process ultimately fails Desjarlais, and he is left without much methodological recourse. (He turns, it should be noted, to theory as a means to irrupt participant meaning-making beyond the confines of experience; Patti Lather [2007] similarly invokes this necessary turn to theory.) However, invoking traditional methodologies is not without productive force. Such activities, it may be surmised, reaffirm the methodological practitioner as a viable citizen in the realm of inquiry; that is, the methodological technocrat risks little by inhabiting a stance built on extraction, desiring methods to better access strategic (normative and legitimated) formations of knowing. Methodologists thus become tour operators with well-worn street maps carefully tucked under each arm. This is the methodologist as middle manager, and the truths s/he tells are extracted truths, commodified and prepackaged for a similarly distanced consumer. Indeed, Certeau (1984) points to the link between normalized ways of knowing and strategic knowledge formations: "Political, economic, and scientific rationality has been constructed on this strategic model" (xix). Obviously, we might add traditional methodological rationality to this potent mix.

In contrast, Certeau's knowledge from below is unregulated and materially situated "through the intricacies of the immediate, the body, the street, the moment, the corporeal senses" (Kenway and Hickey-Moody 2011, 153). This tactical knowledge is risky, as it shifts and changes alongside the terrain, subverting the very processes that enable the reliable order that is traditional methodology. The tactical are improvisational, locationless, spontaneous moments of creativity. There is no "proper place" for tactics, and so they cannot be recognized according to standardized approaches of method; tactics can never be fixed. As Certeau (1984) writes, "without rational transparency, [tactics] are impossible to administer" (93). Working with knowledge from below necessarily refuses any possibility for methodological middle management—the techniques and procedures of method are less stable, not easily prescribed. As a consequence, the very identity of the methodologist is called into question: If not the arbiter of research procedure, how is the methodologist known? What is his/her role within the field? Herein lies an important intersection among Certeau's work on inquiry practices and Foucault's explication of *parrhesia* detailed in Chapter 4: both emphasize ontological and epistemological orientations that subvert the very practices and relations that enable or otherwise mark one as a (methodological) citizen. They are inquiry practices that refuse normalized procedure and operate according to materialist engagements with daily practices of being and knowing: "the body, the street, the moment, the corporeal senses." Formations of tactical knowledge are thus necessarily momentary, linked to the very dynamic relations that constitute the emergent present. In this way traditional methodologies, operating as they do according to logics of extraction, fail any attempt to locate or order the tactical.

As an example of the often-reified interrelation of epistemological assumptions, inquiry practices, and methodological identity, return for a moment to the example of the ease with which the procedurization of extraction promotes a clear, unified, and essentialist vision of *voice*. This voice might be the product of the linear and prescribed research procedure I outlined earlier—the easy movement from interview to recording, to transcript, to codes, to final written text that makes known and interprets a participant's voice. As Mazzei and Youngblood-Jackson (2009) note, "This drive to make voices heard and understood, bringing meaning and self to consciousness and creating transcendental, universal truths, gestures toward the primacy of voice in conventional qualitative research" (1). Through this drive toward the primacy of voice in our methodological work, the concept has lost its material properties. Voice stands in as a metaphor for something else, and yet we so often treat it as though it were a thing-unto-itself. To use Certeau's language, we methodologically claim voice, forgetting that it is but a moveable element, transported from the very material contexts that initiated its creation. That which cannot be cut away—extracted alongside voice—remains outside the field of inquiry, an absence rarely acknowledged in traditional inquiry processes.

In an argument against traditional forms of qualitative research, Youngblood-Jackson and Mazzei (2012) point to the reductive qualities of "mechanistic coding, reducing data to themes, and writing up transparent narratives that do little to critique the complexities of social life" (vii). The over-reliance on such procedurized approaches to research makes possible a type of methodological identity that emphasizes skills of categorization and pinning down knowledge in an effort to "capture" meaning. As Youngblood-Jackson and Mazzei go on to write,

> good methodologists are taught to organize what they have "seen, heard, and read" in order to make sense of and represent what they have learned. Well trained methodologists are carefully taught to be attentive to their field notes and transcription data in order to sort and sift and identify the codes and categories that emerge from the data. (viii)

This stilted form of data management produces legitimated procedures for "making sense" that emphasize necessary reduction in order to locate complete wholes. This is to say that the methodologist-as-data-manager dwells in fixity: fixing meaning in order to fix complete subjects. Though I am not as quick to reject the term *methodologist* as Youngblood-Jackson and Mazzei seem to (they point to their potential positioning as "post-methodologists"), I do value their overt attempts to break the bonds of methodological repetition.

Indeed, traditional formations of method produce something akin to "pure voice"—sound absent the very material properties that make it possible. Voice only becomes recognized and valued through its very production as an object to be defined, known, and "liberated" as some evidence of truth or meaning-making—we create an administratively possible voice so that it might become an object for our analysis. Voice is thus consumed by the interpretive machine, one animated by normalized processes of extraction. As Mazzei and

Youngblood-Jackson (2009) write, "Voice is still 'there' to search for, retrieve, and liberate" (2). Logics of extraction make it there, provide for its retrieval, and make available a host of interpretive analytic processes aimed at its liberation. And yet, like Desjarlais's interrogation of commodified experience, traditional formations of voice occlude the force of removal from a myriad of materially entwined contexts. In many ways this production of materially disengaged voice aligns with Deleuze's (1990) interrogation of the production of sense, wherein sound becomes independent and "ceases to be a quality attached to bodies, a noise or a cry, and … begins to designate qualities, manifest bodies, and signify subjects and predicates" (187). As I have noted elsewhere (Kuntz and Presnall 2012), "the saying of the subject"—its voice—"seems to be the only reality to which we have access" (5). Thus, in order to make new realities possible—new possibilities for being, knowing, and inquiring—we need newly risky methodological approaches that do not operate on such logics of extraction. We need to shift our critical focus from the strategic to the tactical.

In order to enact this shift, critical methodologists thus need to engage in a process Certeau (1984) terms *theoretical questioning,* an interrogative process that never forgets that creating something necessarily excludes other relational possibilities. Certeau distinguishes between *individual science* and *theoretical questioning,* noting that the former dwells in the practice of experimentation and is thus a process of bringing silences into language, of verbalizing things within their own *a priori* field (61). Individual science and its subsequent silencing practices is the province of standardized method (recall here those standardized research practices that produce "voice" and interpret it for the consumer, all the while silencing those material relations from which it extends). Theoretical questioning, on the contrary, always keeps in memory the "remainder" of ordinary practices (that which does not speak) and refuses to operate under a *logic of extraction.* Theoretical questioning dwells in knowledges from below—materially situated and politically engaged—refusing, in this case, the separation of sound from bodies, voice from material circumstance.

I should pause here a moment to note that much has been made of the relation of qualitative inquiry to science, particularly in response to policy documents that seek to normalize particular definitions of scientific research and requisite practices (e.g., *Qualitative Inquiry*'s dedicated issues after the production of the National Research Council's Report: Cannella and Lincoln 2004; Lincoln and Cannella 2004). These responses have come in multiple formations, and there is no need for me to play them out here. However, I do want to recognize Certeau's displacement of individual science—a silencing practice that can only speak to itself—in favor of the more materialist practices inherent in theoretical questioning. And I also want to recognize how a shift away from inquiry-as-individual science resists what Ian Stronach (2010) terms the "neo-positivist counter revolution" in methodological work (5). In this sense it is not whether qualitative inquiry is scientific but rather that critical practices of inquiry need to openly resist the seductions of individual science in favor of a more productive—and materially relational—stand inherent in theoretical questioning.

In some ways, then, Mazzei and Youngblood-Jackson's (2009) text may be read as an attempt to resist traditional approaches to voice via individual science in favor of theoretically questioning. Theirs is an invitation to consider more risky engagements with voice, risky approaches that I read as stemming from a newfound consideration of methodological responsibility. In alignment with the theoretical questioning put forth by Mazzei and Youngblood-Jackson, we might strive to understand voice before its easy extraction; indeed, voice embedded within material context—rather than extracted and interpreted from without—may not be voice at all: new possibilities emerge in such lines of flight away from traditional formations of the subject, voice, and experience. If we learn from Desjarlais (1997) that "some people sometimes live in terms different from experience" (18), we can here perhaps wonder how some people sometimes speak or make known in terms different from voice. And such critical interrogations, engaged theoretical questioning, perhaps begin with the refusal of extraction, the recognition of the materiality of our methodological work.

It is this remainder—or the residue of daily practices inherent in theoretical questioning—to which we might turn our methodological attention, the traces of the everyday that are not immediately governed (or consumed) by the trappings of normative *logics of extraction*. This work is decidedly materialist and, in Certeau's (1984) words, stems from "Linking acts and footsteps, opening meanings and directions" in order to make visible "liberated spaces that can be occupied" (105). Of course, this is not easy work, especially as it requires a shift away from normalized epistemological and ontological assumptions. We need to *know, come to know,* and *be* differently in order to make visible those material spaces of liberation. Further, we need to make possible newly relational approaches that resist confinement—materialist methodological work that continues to exceed itself. The rest of this book seeks to provide a space for such critical work, to nudge and prod critical inquirers to take seriously the work of theoretical questioning in the research practices they enact, the committees they engage, and the classes they teach.

Logics of Extraction and Social Justice Work

Framing methodological identity (as technocrat) and responsibility (as concerned with procedural matters) alongside *logics of extraction* offers select possibilities concerning matters of change and social justice. Indeed, I wonder what potential for change lies within *logics of extraction?* If contemporary logic formations privilege an expertise of technique even as they situate the methodologist as a middle manager of data, change perhaps only happens at the level of procedure and outputs. As a consequence, the methodologist in this scenario has responsibility for activating change only at the level of his/her expertise. This seems remarkably limiting.

Given traditional approaches to research as outlined in this chapter, extractivist research in the name of social justice would seem to privilege those acts that "free" the individual subject from the binds of context. This might include assumed neoliberal values of hyper-individualism as well as defining the subject outside of contextual relation (and, thus, unencumbered or "free"). This has manifested, for example, in a liberal privileging of voice (as individual, as discrete, as separable) and experience (as linearly progressive change to a coherent and definable subject) as having intrinsic methodological value. In this instance, methodologists have gone to great lengths to isolate and give discrete definition to voice over and against the dissonance of context.

Further, much work has been done to "give voice" to individuals from underrepresented or marginalized groups. Again, this is not to say that attempts to isolate and/or give voice to others are inherently negative; instead, such acts are dangerous, and this danger manifests in particular ways. To "give voice" is to mistake a process for a commodity—I give you something you did not previously have (or would no longer have were it not for my methodological intervention). Further, this act of subjective charity reinscribes select power hierarchies wherein I reproduce my position of power (as the marker of legitimate voice) and the powerless position of the other (one who needs methodological legitimation to claim a voice). However, though dangerous, such methodological practices are hardly risky. Traditional research orientations toward extracting voice prescribe a series of legitimated coding strategies that systematically separate subjects from relational context (producing a discrete subject that can be known and showing that subject as visible/knowable within a select research project) and reframe that subject's voice as meaningful within extracted contexts. The most explicit example of this is the tripartite coding strategy that developed as part of the codification of grounded theory and has now achieved a ubiquitous status in qualitative inquiry. Here, thematic codes are isolated within transcripts (open coding), those codes are then understood in relation to one another (axial coding), and the most salient codes are then selected for further explication within the body of the research paper (selective coding). Importantly, this process is often offered as somehow natural, and the subject-voice that is confected via the process is given privileged status as holding some known truth. This is commodification and reification in the name of social justice. Yet we might find value in a different sense of methodological risk and responsibility.

Following the interpretive orientation offered by Davies (2010), a critique of rational systems such as neoliberalism "makes visible the way in which individuals are caught up in the events of their time, often unable to see where those events are taking them, or how they might think otherwise" (56). Similarly, I offer a critique of neoliberalism and globalization to show the ways in which such governing systems catch methodologists "up in the events of their time," unable to think differently (what Deleuze [1995] would term *difference*) and only to engage in repetition. To productively continue this critique, I turn in the next chapter to a materialist framework that might usefully intervene in the *logic of extraction*, making space for methodological possibilities with implications for social justice.

Chapter 3

Materialism and Critical Materialism

Introduction

Given my overview of extractivist logics, globalized neoliberalism, and traditional qualitative research in Chapter 2, I next set out to (re)consider such issues within a materialist framework with particularly promising effects for qualitative inquiry in the name of social justice. To begin, it remains important to note that neoliberalism and globalization have very material effects—these perspectives do not simply exist in theory; they impact the material contexts through which we live our lives. The globalized neoliberal context has a hand in how we interpret, understand, engage within, and feel about the world in which we live. *Logics of extraction* encourage particular readings of such circumstances, even as they disavow select ways of coming to know as irrelevant or otherwise unnecessary. In response, a focus on the material impact of such processes makes newly available select inquiry practices and possibilities that are not beholden to the value-laden assumptions of extractive logics. Operating according to *logics of extraction* brings with it superficial ethical stances regarding methodological risk and responsibility. Shifting away from such logics makes available newly emergent formations of these key terms and practices; it changes what we do as critical methodologists, why we do it, and it makes available emergent

The Responsible Methodologist: Inquiry, Truth-Telling, and Social Justice, by Aaron M. Kuntz, 61–91.
© 2015 Left Coast Press, Inc. All rights reserved.

possibilities for yet-to-be-recognized daily practices of living. As a result, new possibilities for inquiry as social justice work become available. Whereas extractivist logics emphasize a responsibility for distance, relational approaches foreground an ethic of disruption and intervention *within* the contexts that grant them their visibility or definition. As such, there remains an important intersection among materialist approaches to inquiry, considerations of affect (what some deem the "affective turn" in social analysis), and overtly engaged ethical stances regarding methodological risk and responsibility.

Given our contemporary fixation on *logics of extraction*—outlined in Chapter 2—it remains important to establish ways for countering such constraining methodological circumstances. That is, I want to utilize this chapter to consider alternative ways of knowing and coming to know, with the assumption that such possibilities create alternative ways of being. As alluded to in the opening sections of this book, I find promise in epistemological and ontological formations that remain steeped in material circumstances and context. In short, I propose materialist methodologies as a way to reconsider what it means to be methodologically responsible and a renewed appreciation for methodological risk. As such, I organize this section by first considering materialism from the perspective of dialectical relations and attendant implications for inquiry. From dialectical relations I draw from the promise of relational thinking that is more dialogic in order, with particular considerations for the question of voice and silence in qualitative inquiry. Next I offer a sense of critical materialism as in line with what many scholars now term the *new materialism* in social science and educational research. I end by linking inquiry as social justice work with a materialist approach to research, pointing to the promise of *parrhesia* as explicated in Chapter 4. The result, I hope, is a sense of materialist activism that gives renewed purpose to the work of inquiry.

Methodological Mad-Libs and the Work of Theory

Because extractivist logic is often assumed within educational research (and is thus indicative of its normative status) approaches to inquiry are rendered in limited ways, beginning as they do from a standpoint of contextual differentiation. This leads Peim (2009) to locate the problem of how theory is simplistically depicted within contemporary research texts:

> Educational research handbooks frequently provide a kind of theory menu for the would-be researcher to use as a guide. Choose your orientation, produce

your design, gather your data, set your mode of interpretation, produce findings, and then—display and disseminate. Research choices are often presented in the form of binaries that define methodology: quantitative or qualitative, positivist or constructivist, enlightenment or postmodern. (236)

I would add assumptions of linearity to Peim's recognition of the theory menu as an oversimplified methodological guidebook: most often there are prescribed steps that assume movement from one choice to the next in a progressive motion toward research enactment and completion. This closed formation of research steps seems (uneasily) familiar, resembling a "choose your own adventure" sequencing of theory-to-design-to-data-to-interpretation-to-findings-to-dissemination.

When I was a kid, I used to consume the *choose your own adventure* series of books. These are the stories with sections and chapters that ask the reader to make a choice for the main characters and proceed to corresponding pages; in this scenario the reader feels a degree of agency, as though s/he had a hand in the outcome of the story. As an adolescent, I loved the nervous feeling of coming to a conclusion on behalf of the protagonist and being told to turn to page 35, say, to see the outcome of my decision. Of course, adolescent that I was, I also cheated—keeping a finger on the page where I was asked to make the decision in case I made the wrong one and needed to go back and right my mistaken selection. I'm not sure this can so easily be done regarding questions of inquiry, particularly around issues of social justice. So herein lies an interesting question: At what point can we go back and remake select methodological (inquiry) decisions within the inquiry process? Or at what point in the inquiry process have we come too far to (re)make methodologically informed/determined choices? When do select choices foreclose other possibilities? I suggest that assuming extractivist logics situates the methodologist on a narrowed path toward reductive, simplistic findings that have little hope for producing progressive social change.

Given the reductive confines that come with unquestioned acceptance of extractivist logic, the *choose your own adventure* metaphor, though resonate with my own adolescent experiences, is probably not as apt as that of *methodological Mad-Libs*: insert your theoretical frame here, your methods there, and your findings over there. Logics of extraction provide the structure for the game—you just fill in the blanks. Unlike traditional *Mad-Libs* (which prove humorous due to their nonsensical result), the goal of *methodological Mad-Libs* would be to produce a wholly rational result, one that squares with the doctrines of common sense and normative rationality. Perhaps the role of theory—or critical intervention—is to make presentations of methodological *Mad-Libs* laughable once again, to show the contradictory or otherwise limiting logic structures that form contemporary regimes of truth. To paraphrase Georges Canguilhem (1991), the goal of theory in this sense is not to solve problems; it is to cause them.

Working Against Comfort

We live in fluid times. We make meaning from multiple directions and in multiple directions from a very early age and are affected by this meaning-making process. These are relational ways of engaging with the world. Yet for some reason we come to understand more formalized (or academic) ways of making meaning as acts that necessarily stop the fluidity of everyday life. In positivistic times research was engaged to stop meaning from moving—to capture a stasis that could be reliably (and repeatedly) shown as still. In postpositivistic times research perhaps sought to create a "snapshot" of meaning, with the recognition that meaning is created and, through its creation, moves. This is, I suppose, the invocation of stasis for conceptual clarity. Up to this point the research activity—and those who activated that activity—remained outside the phenomena of interest, engaging designs and instruments to capture meaning from a distance. With this present chapter's focus on materialism, both old and new, we are offered a critique of extractive meaning-making through what some term the *Cartesian cut* (see Barad 2007, 2012). Taking its meaning from the philosophy of science, the Cartesian cut establishes the subject from the object, thus enabling particular practices of meaning-making—with, of course, particular consequences. Through separating the subject from the object—making them externally relatable—meaning is produced through segmentation and isolation; removing phenomena from their relations and subsequent processes. In this sense we now have a progressively layered process of inquiry, one informed by the *logic of extraction* and made manifest by the Cartesian cut. A materialist approach to inquiry critiques this historically normative process of inquiry and perhaps affords us a new orientation toward knowing, coming to know, and being, one operating according to relational logics that inform meaning-making as an entangled, unfinished event.

With materialist methodologies we begin to see inquiry as actively engaged in the ongoing production of meaning—an encounter and productive relation within the phenomena of interest. More simply stated, materialist methodologies begin with the assumption that engaging in inquiry practices always affects the phenomena of interest—we can never *not* impact that which we study. As a result, there is no distance between inquirer and "data"—meaning is made within, not examined from without. This begins with the assumption that once phenomena are captured—made to be still and thereby outside of the processual—they are no longer what they once were: through stasis they cease to be productively relational; they become things.[1] Research, then, makes things from relations, extracted objects cut off from meaning.[2]

Working within the assumed stasis of knowledge that extends from post/positivistic approaches to inquiry makes possible select comforts. There is the comfortable space, for example, of *certainty,* wherein one achieves levels of knowing that exist outside of—or beyond—question. We know because the data tell us so. There is also, I suppose, the comfort of *causation*: this identified cause led to this recognizable effect. If we alter the particular cause in intentional ways, we can produce these anticipated effects. Lastly, operating according to *logics of extraction*—as post/positivistic approaches to research do—extends the comfort of *prescription*: valid research is directional, pointing toward actions and/or practices with consistent outcomes across time and space. In this way such research has a seductive quality—given contemporary cultural values, who would not want the comforts of certainty, causation, and prescription? Further still, given the rather fragmented disorientation that seems to be our postmodern condition, who could object to easing our social anxiety with the balm of neatly ordered inquiry?

Materialist approaches to inquiry eschew the logical comforts of extraction—and the anxieties that extend from the inevitable traces of researcher presence—in favor of more ambiguous spaces of uncertainty. Dwelling within the contextual immediate, materialist inquiry necessarily gives up claims for certainty, inferences of causation, and goals of prescription; instead, materially grounded methodologies dwell within the momentary constellations of meaning of which they themselves are a part. Such an approach to knowing remains ensconced in the event of the now, becoming with the phenomena they seek to understand, never outside the meanings they work to produce. As a result, even as the materialist methodologist relinquishes the privilege of full or complete knowledge, s/he also releases the anxiety of influence—concerns about affecting data or findings fall away as objectivity and/or neutrality cease to be justifiable goals. Methodological responsibility is reconstituted away from the epistemic privileging of distance; instead, a performative dialogic relation within phenomenal events makes possible the productive relation of knowing *with* being. Through knowing differently we come to be differently. Through being differently we come to newly productive knowledges. All of these collapsed relations make possible alternative possibilities for inquiry in the name of social justice.

In order to extract, one must recognize an external environment into which such extraction might extend. For those logic structures that have come to dominate traditional qualitative research, this extraction is made possible by an adherence to Cartesian assumptions regarding absolute time and space—both entities are identified as objective and fixed. In this sense time and space coincide as a static entity against which other things and relations might be measured. As a result, the Cartesian cut exists through maintaining an easy division between the measured and the instrument that measures, the object and the measuring subject. Meaning is thus made through this cut, through the separation of the known from the knower. In the laboratory this simply means that the technology (say, a microscope) necessarily remains distinct from the element it inspects (say, a water sample). Meaning occurs through the active separation of the water sample (the object) from the microscope (the instrument that measures or otherwise makes the object visible). However, when my eleven-year-old pulls out his microscope, he recognizes that its light—intended to illuminate the water sample—warms the slide that, in turn, activates the sample in potentially interesting ways. Some might deem this light-based activation problematic (and, I suppose, something to be overcome with more or better technology); he just thinks it's neat. As an untrained scientist, he has yet to learn the scientific requirement of parceling out effects—he reads the entire relation (the water engaged with the light's warmth with the slide, etc.) as an ongoing phenomena; scientific purity is not (yet) his aim. Traditionally, of course, we have deemed any (measurable) impact of the microscope on the element as contamination. We look to manage any site of contamination, to mitigate it, in a quest for more certain distinctions—causation, certainty, and prescription once again rule the day.

Within the social sciences similar claims stem from assertions of the Cartesian cut. This extends from a belief that, in qualitative research, the researcher "is the instrument" through which meaning is made, insinuating that the researcher-as-instrument necessarily remains separate from the phenomenon s/he interprets; the researcher manages and embodies the "cut" through which meaning is made. The researcher is the subject; the researched the object. As a result, like in the laboratory, a vast array of technologies and research practices extend from desires to maintain the Cartesian cut, to make possible and maintain the division between instrument and researcher (thereby making manifest "clear" or uncontaminated findings). Often in my classes this manifests in ongoing questions about the possibility that students will somehow bias the interview by asserting their own interpretations of reality onto/into their research project. The thought seems to be that recognition of bias will disavow the Cartesian cut, foreclosing attempts to separate subjects from contexts, the necessary isolation of knowledge from the knower—this would result, of course, in the discomfort of nonclarity. Like my son's microscope and its contaminating light, one works to control or even eliminate the impact of the one on the other; the purity of separation is what must be attained.

Yet what is so wrong with contamination? Why must it be dealt with so severely through a host of technologies and practices? What might be lost in our attempts to contain or otherwise discipline contamination?

Drop a bit of food coloring into clear liquid and the entire entity displays its effect: notice the short time it takes for the once-easy distinction between color and transparent solution to fade, losing significance as the edges of the one blur into the other. The color dissipates slightly, simultaneously fading from the point of contact and coloring that which it impacts. If purity was our goal, or the ability to separate one from another and examine them independently, then this becomes harder with the passage of time as the liquids continue their encounter. Once discernible boundaries lose their edge, as does the ability to state what is within and what remains without. One can no longer easily distinguish the drop from the solution, the cause from its effect. In many ways, then, these dynamic qualities provide a methodological quandary: How to conceptually engage with such ambiguity? Yet if we soften our gaze a bit, no longer looking for the hard edges of distinction, one might make meaning differently—no longer fixated upon principles of differentiation, we perhaps develop an openness to the multiple ways in which such encounters produce select resonances.

I have written previously (Kuntz 2011b) about the potential for critical qualitative inquiry to serve as a productive irritant, activating normative processes to excited visibility and change. Pulling from the means by which the irritant and normative function affect one another through a critical encounter, I noted how irritation makes visible those systemic processes that sustain normative formations and assumptions that remain otherwise unnoticed. As a social irritant, materialist inquiry might make visible what otherwise would remain unacknowledged (though no less impactful). Mine was, I suppose, a call for critical intervention, one that drew from the more biological metaphor of an organism stimulated to overt action. The irritant metaphor appeals to me because it has a material basis and, as such, emphasizes a relational means of knowing: the organism encounters the irritant and responds, enflamed to overt action. In that moment of response the irritant and organism are not so easily distinguished—in the moment of irritation the two coalesce within the response. Though I did not at the time explore the intra-active[3] possibilities of the relation—and though the irritant metaphor will inevitably fall short (as all metaphors do)—I want in this chapter to further develop the material relationality that extends from the metaphor and do so with an eye toward the possibility of enacting critical qualitative inquiry for progressive social change. In order to do so we must begin with considerations for relational ways of thinking, knowing, and being that disrupt our historical adherence to extractive logics and traditional methodologies.

Relational Thinking, Knowing, Being

In discussions with both students and colleagues I have been frustrated to hear qualitative inquiry critiqued as "merely descriptive." That is, there is a persistent belief that the goal of qualitative inquiry is to re-present particular contexts whether they be more locally or globally situated. Such a summation necessarily relies on an *a priori* assumption that research can stand outside, describing that of which it is distinctly *not* a part. I respond to such determinations by asserting that good qualitative inquiry does more than describe; it *intervenes* on multiple material levels. Oftentimes such interventions occur through disrupting common-sensical interpretations of reality and the daily practices they inform. Further, such interventions are never one-time events but rather occur in-process and imply an ethical stance against status quo injustices. The critical qualitative researcher positions him/herself within contexts in which daily acts of inquiry can bring about change. In this way critical qualitative inquiry implies particular ontological, epistemological, and ethical alignments within the world that cannot coexist with extractive logic.

The expression of the limited descriptive qualities of qualitative research extends, I suppose, from notions of events or happenings as *products,* with clear markers for a beginning and an ending. In this line of thought, qualitative research describes, as precisely as possible, some construed reality that has already occurred—inquiry as retrospectively descriptive. The "merely" in the antiquated phrase "merely descriptive" stems from the juxtaposed qualities of more quantitatively aligned work that does not rest in description; it predicts. This system of logic results in my well-intentioned colleagues good-naturedly assuring me that they encourage their students to engage in qualitative work in order to better "know" an event so as to better inform their more-structured quantitative studies. As one colleague mentioned to me, "You have to know before you can test—qualitative studies help me with that knowing."

I want to be clear that it is not the use or nonuse of quantitative methods that I am questioning here; rather, it is the system of logic that understands social reality and human meaning-making as decidedly static and inquiry as mere re-presentations of the status quo. More than producing descriptions of static contexts, critical qualitative inquiry intervenes in social processes with the aim of instigating change. As a critical qualitative researcher, I engage in inquiry as a social justice act, as a means for inciting change in social institutions and processes, not, it should be noted, to change individuals to fit those institutions.

To that end I begin each semester in my introductory qualitative research course with a simple PowerPoint slide that reads: *The purpose of educational inquiry is to improve the human condition.* I am not so sure I believe such improvements can occur through simple description nor through systems of logic that are built on a series of extractions. So I turn instead to intervention.

The *Oxford English Dictionary* defines the verb "intervene" to mean "to come in as something extraneous, in the course of some action, state of things, etc." (intervention). It is the extraneousness of intervention that I find interesting—that it begins as in excess to an action or state. Interventions thus point to an openness, an extension of actions and states that might otherwise continue on in a closed-loop fashion. In this way intervention is productive—making new spaces where previously there had been none.

As the *Oxford English Dictionary* goes on to note, that which intervenes dwells in indeterminate spaces, situating itself between other things: intervention is "to lie between" events, times, or actions—intervention as indeterminate excess, dwelling in the interstices among the entanglements of context. And, as I noted earlier, such interventions need to be processual in order. Thus, it is not a moment or act of intervention but a process of intervening that is on my mind. Intervention may occur in the gaps or fractures of otherwise "complete" processes. What, then, does thinking in terms of processes provide the inquirer? How might the processual infer a relational perspective that decidedly counters extractivist logics?

To begin, relational thinking posits a frame of knowing and coming to know that can no longer adhere to the principles of subject-object that extend from the Cartesian cut. Meaning develops within relations—there is no mechanism to constitute meaning outside relations. Put another way, there is no meaning to be made "unto itself," cut free from or absent relation. There are, instead, an overdetermined array of entangled relations, and it is this incessant relationality that makes possible a materially situated yet constantly moving knowledge, conceptions of meaning that are decidedly not fixed or static. Perhaps an example is in order here, one that emphasizes the relational orientation toward knowing that extends from a materialist methodological approach to inquiry.

In order to understand how a relationally oriented materialism might productively inform critical approaches to inquiry, one first has to think differently from the logics criticized in the previous chapter. In contradistinction, a materialist framework operates on *relational* presumptions about knowing and being that trouble normative categories such as inside/outside and internal/external. Often productive methodological examples of moving toward a materialist relationality might be found in those inquiry projects that foreground issues of embodiment and emplacement. I previously noted the ways in which Desjarlais's *Shelter Blues* disrupts normative methodological and theoretical processes through refusing the standardized *humanist subject.* Desjarlais puts this theorization into play through an insistence on materialist analyses of participants' bodies relationally implicated by the contours of the homeless shelter they frequent, the sociopolitical policies surrounding sanity and abnormality, and Westernized productions of the self, to name but a few of the relations found in the text. Importantly, these relations are caught up within one another, never fully distinguishable, and always material. Thus it is that Desjarlais reveals the historical production of the shelter itself (placed within a building influenced by postmodern architecture), economic policies (that result in the building remaining incomplete due to budget cuts), the embodied meaning of homelessness (of being outside the pace of time, of inhabiting indeterminate spaces), and the pressures of sense-making (of claiming a coherent *I*, of rendering oneself as contained and distinct) as caught up within the event of inquiry. An ongoing materialist relationality drives Desjarlais's work, requiring him to consider his own material responsibilities within the very relations he considers in his text.

Along similar lines, Loic Wacquant's (2004) *Body & Soul* foregrounds processes of embodiment to make possible a relational materiality through which we encounter the world. As such, Wacquant strives for a methodological approach that stems "*from* the body, that is, deploying the body as a tool of inquiry and vector of knowledge" (viii, original emphasis). Through his determination to situate the body as a means for coming-to-know, Wacquant refuses a methodological tradition of establishing the body as a thing to be analyzed, made known via descriptive containment. Here Wacquant "takes seriously, at the theoretical, methodological, and rhetorical levels, the fact that the social agent is before anything else a being of flesh, nerves, and senses ... who partakes of the universe that makes him, and that he in turn contributes to making, with every fiber of his heart" (vii). This approach foregrounds a relational materiality that is not possible given the assumed separations of extractive logics. Materialist approaches require dynamically relational ways of knowing, coming to know, and being.

New materialists extend the relational knowing depicted in such examples and follow it to important conclusions regarding the collapse of knowing into being (from easy distinctions between the epistemic and ontic to onto-episte-mological assertions of the world). As such, new materialists might productively extend Desjarlais's collapse of embodiment and emplacement with the self or Wacquant's notion of the body as a relational tool for meaning-making by perhaps reorganizing how such material relations occur within phenomena, not as a means to generate data that exist without. However, it is important to note that this shift in thinking is not a function of some historical trajectory of linear progression: we thought this way a hundred years ago, that way fifty years ago, and now, in all of our contemporary awareness, we think this particular way. History need not be read in such limiting linear ways. Indeed, as I try to show throughout the intersection of the chapters of this book, the materialist perspective of Marxism overlaps with the new materialisms of contemporary time that, in turn, overlap with assumptions of truth-telling advocated by the Ancient Greeks and is, of course, rerecognized by the poststructural perspective of Foucault in the 1980s. Assumptions about being and knowing are far from ordered and detailed; they extend, branch out through time and space, and in-form a host of practices and perspectives throughout the world. Thus, this book seeks not so much to disentangle the skein of philosophical assumptions as it does to map particular philosophical perspectives on to one another in order to consider the implications on method and inquiry, respectively. Perhaps one of the more useful ways to work our way through this is to consider how different ways of thinking about and being in the world made sense of—or overcome in particular ways—the inevitable contradictions that extend throughout their orientation.

Relational Thinking and Processual Analysis

Understanding the world as composed relationally makes possible particular approaches to analysis. Importantly, a materialist analysis asks questions that are necessarily previous to those offered by research approaches governed by *logics of extraction* and Cartesian cuts—more contemporary formations of materialism do not begin with assumptions of fixed difference. Instead of locat-ing objects through distancing practices, a materialist analysis might usefully examine how historical practices of "cutting" to make meaning have taken on the onus of common sense, assumed patterns of meaning-making. Such pat-terns become enmeshed in an ongoing series of relationships that, when aligned, make visible sets of material processes that we have perhaps come to take for granted as necessarily "real."

Following the Marxian notion that our social world is a dynamic series of relationships, Resnick and Wolff (1987) assert "process" as a basic unit of materialist analysis. In establishing their methodological means for inquiry, the authors note, "every relationship in society is composed of its distinguishing set of processes" (19). As such, the critical inquirer might examine the repeated ways in which select relationships historically form as a series of sociopolitical—and decidedly material—processes. Importantly these processes are *over-determined*—they consist of an endless array of conjoined relation:

> Each social process is the effect produced by the interaction of … all the others. . . . Thus, each social process, understood as overdetermined, is conceived as contradictory. It is the site of influences from all other social processes that push and pull it in all sorts of ways. Its overdetermination constitutes the process's existence and its internal tensions. These produce its movement, its change. (24)

To cut relationships from their overdetermined processes is to stop their movement, to engage in meaning-making through manufactured fixity. Further, to attempt analysis through presumed fixity is to reinforce an essentialistic rendering of the world: through asserting stasis on an ever-changing series of processes one presumes an essence to the relations. The essence is then drawn out (cut) from overdetermined contexts and privileged above all others.

Instead, one might begin from a discernible and overt entry point for analysis (Resnick and Wolff 1987). This is the means by which one enters into an understanding of select processes, intentionally selecting relations of meaning-making for the benefit of critical intervention. Keeping in mind that assumptions of overdetermination preclude portraying any one entry point as having greater determining effects than any other process, the importance lies in an ability to make one's entry point visible and an extension of deliberate critique—rather than simply the inevitable result of methodological prescription. Further, the act of making visible one's entry point productively entangles the inquirer with the process of inquiry—there can be no pretensions of distancing oneself from the processes one studies.

In addition to the emphasis on overdetermination and entry points of analysis that extend from the neo-Marxist materialism of Resnick and Wolff (1987), my advocacy for processual analyses draws from Renato Rosaldo's (1993) interrogation of social analysis within cultural anthropology. Rosaldo's "remaking of social analysis" (which is the subtitle of his book) paves the way for productively distinguishing between two ways of coming to know and acting through knowing: *relativistic* and *relational* onto-epistemologies.[4] Thinking in terms of ongoing and dynamically related processes shifts the terrain away from concerns of relativism that are all too simplistically lobbed at more poststructural approaches to knowledge formation. In place of relativism, Rosaldo's processual approach points toward a relational responsibility that usefully informs methodological work.

As a disengaged and rudderless approach to inquiry, relativism makes absent any possibility for understanding the interrelation of systems, processes, or practices. This is the "I have my culture/way of knowing and you have yours" approach. Many critics of contemporary theory have utilized a superficial and simplistic reading of postmodern social thought to conflate postmodernism with relativism. If, such critics might ask, there exist no independent truths or externally existent objects (as postmodern theorists might claim)—if all things are overdetermined—then how does one make any worthwhile claims about the world? How does one move beyond the immobilized default stance of "It's all relative—who am I to say what another should or should not do"? This is, of course, to mistakenly conflate relational thinking with a type of moral relativism that has no grounding for action within the sociocultural world.

Epistemologically, relativism reinforces particularistic ways of coming to know—as though no knowledge can be extended beyond the immediate environment in which it is made manifest. This, in turn, leads to a degree of ontological disengagement and disinterestedness. In short, if I believe that my experiences do not extend beyond my immediate locale, I have little moral or ethical justification to comment upon or intervene in events or practices that exceed my local contexts. This perhaps leads to incessant navel-gazing (admittedly a problem in the academy), as I can only rightly examine or critique my own experience. I note this as a simplistic reading of postmodern thought because it mistakes fragmentation for isolation and confuses partial knowledge formations for the inability to act in any political way. The point of relational assumptions about the world is not that all things are relative and therefore I have no right to intervene in other relations; it is, indeed, quite the opposite. *Because I am forever in-relation, I have a responsibility to engage; I am never free to pretend a disassociated stance.* As noted earlier, I also have a responsibility to make visible my entry point for engagement—that I choose to engage with these processes in these ways because I value these elements. This is materialist work, always returning to (and operating from) identified material relations and contexts. In order to make visible my entry point, I have an additional responsibility for interrogating my own justification for the claims I make—I cannot rest on the laurels of some fixed procedure for coming to know.

Through this materialist approach to inquiry, I maintain a distinction between particular and partial knowledge. Following the tenor of the *Oxford English Dictionary*, the *particular* emphasizes a distinct, single, individual element "apart from the rest" (particular). In contrast, *partial* insinuates incompleteness, a "relation of the part to a larger whole" (partial). These definitions point to an important distinction between relativism's overemphasis on *particular* knowledge formations (my experience is distinct, disengaged, and set apart from others) and more postmodern relational conceptions of *partial* knowledge formations (this incomplete understanding stands forever in relation to larger sociohistorical contexts that can never be fully ignored). Equally as important, the disengaged separateness emblematic of relativistic thinking most often translates to an "I'll do me and you do you" claim of ethical independence.

On the contrary, the contemporary theory I find most insightful refuses relativistic ways of knowing and coming to know in favor of more relational onto-epistemological stances and ethical imperatives. The distinction here remains important: whereas *relativism* leads to separateness and detachment, *relationality* necessitates a dynamic connection between all acts of knowing, doing, and becoming. Thus, our assumptions about how we know and what we might do with that knowledge are never divorced from the larger, more macro-level issues that otherwise might be thought to exceed us. Importantly, thinking along relational lines allows us to link local-level practices and analyses with more global debates that are never fully detached from our everyday practices. Relational thinking makes possible an activist stance that requires an ethical engagement with multiple and varied contexts—we never exist outside of relation to anything or anyone else. Following Bennett's (2010) emphasis on relational materiality, as articulated in her explication of thing-theory, I am interested in the "sense of a melting of cause and effect" (33), wherein notions of causality and agency are more emergent than fixed, more fluid than stable.

A useful example here extends from the insidious nature of globalization, discussed in the previous chapter. Relationally speaking, I cannot fully separate the ongoing anxieties of falling behind the larger world order or maintaining an economically productive and competitive workforce within the city of Birmingham, Alabama (where I live as I write this), from larger issues and debates that affect factory workers in China, for example, or socialist activists in Venezuela. Nor can I completely divorce my daily practices from principles of hyper-individualism, surveillance, and economic determinism that so easily extend from a neoliberal sensibility and feed processes of globalization. To do so would be to extract myself from the very discourses that encourage particular readings of my actions and subjectivities (the thought, for example, that "good citizens" are those who can ably contribute to the international economy or that "who I am" is determined by my occupation; on the latter issue, consider the ease with which we seek to know people through asking "what they do"—meaning, what is their occupation? Here, occupation stands in for identity, who a person is).

This shift to relationality has important implications for inquiry. Refusing to take on simplistic renditions of relativism means that I cannot separate methodological means for coming to know from assumptions regarding what can be known and what we might do with that knowledge. Consequently, if I solely engage in and reproduce traditional methodological means for coming to know (the traditional interview, say, or the objective observation) I, at the same time, re-invoke the very assumptions that make such a methodological approach available from the beginning. Further, if I consider myself as someone who works for progressive change through inquiry (and I do), then I must necessarily recognize how my very inquiry practices, in many ways, gain meaning from the larger neoliberal and globalized discourses I seek to counter. In this sense relational thinking opens the possibility for methodological strategies that link more macro-level discursive patternings (say, globalized neoliberalism) with more micro-level and localized practices. Thus, my research must attend to the many ways in which the values of globalized neoliberalism give a sense of meaning to my everyday practices (making them visible and sensical in our contemporary age) even as my more localized activities reinscribe (or, perhaps, are assumed within) the manufactured values that are neoliberal in order. As such, I perhaps have a responsibility to locate and problematize such connections. Never entirely distinct, our practices and governing rationalities perpetually (re)create one another anew within multiple contexts.

Importantly, relational thinking brings with it an ethical and moral obligation that relativism does not. Once we become aware of our connections to multiple discourses, we might be said to, at the same time, become responsible for their resolution. Pushing beyond an ethic of disruption (one that perhaps seeks to impede the normative flow of knowing and coming to know), we now have a newfound responsibility to construct methodologies that attend to relational formations of knowing and being—a responsibility that addresses epistemological and ontological concerns. Consequently, relational thinking might be seen to activate and enable social justice work, asking that we work for social change even as we, ourselves, are open to being changed by such work. Again, returning to the emphasis on inquiry for a moment, relational thinking makes possible the recognition that how we inquire matters—the means by which we come to our knowledge, has implications for what we do with that knowledge, making possible (or not) a vision of inquiry-for-social-justice. This is because our inquiry methods themselves are part of the overdetermined processes we seek to analyze. It is my hope that relational thinking makes possible an activist stance that requires an ethical engagement with multiple and varied contexts.

An ongoing engagement with processes brings with it the concomitant valuing of fluidity over fixity, movement over stasis, and relational change as a matter of course. By definition, a *process* implies that change occurs; processes can never be static. Processes can replay the same things over and over, but even within such replication they engage change, though from a distanced perspective, they may appear fixed.

As an example, when traveling down the interstate, I have often encountered an odd phenomenon—looking over to the car next to me, it appears that its hubcaps fail to move. Though I am cognizant that I (and presumably the car next to me) am traveling at a speed of nearly seventy miles per hour, the hubcaps seem perfectly still. They move, of course, but they have achieved the perfect speed of rotation so as to appear still (this is also, as an aside, how old fluorescent lights and television screens worked—flickering at such a rapid pace that the human eye misinterprets that they are always on). Transfer this rather mundane experience to the element of the social, and this might usefully explain why social processes appear static or fixed as well as how something as fluid as power may appear to reside within individuals or locales. Through intensive circulation what otherwise would be known as in flux seems constant or still. Processual analyses acknowledge this phenomenon even as they begin from the assumption that processes invoke change. In order to gain access to—or productively intervene within—such processes, we might begin with a critical interrogation of daily material practices.

Material Practices

At times the theoretical shift from a reliance on fixity (and Cartesian cuts for knowledge formation) to more relational ways of knowing and coming to know can (usefully) complicate or challenge traditional methodological approaches. Given such theoretical assertions, where does one begin the inquiry process? That is, how does one inquire into processes that forever move, are never complete, and are relationally known? To borrow from my previous example, when it comes to traditional inquiry approaches, a significant amount of methodological energy has gone into establishing hubcaps as fixed and therefore fully knowable/measureable without the rather critical recognition that they travel at seventy miles per hour down the highway.

In response, I follow Foucault, who insisted on an examination of practices as an entry point for analysis. As Foucault (1991) notes, his

> target of analysis wasn't "institutions", "theories" or "ideology", but practices—with the aim of grasping the conditions which make these acceptable at a given moment; the hypothesis being that these types of practice ... possess up to a point their own specific regularities, logic, strategy, self-evidence and "reason"... practices being understood here as places where what is said and what is done, rules imposed and reasons given, the planned and the taken for granted meet and interconnect. (75)

In this sense daily practices reveal the larger social processes and rationalities that make them possible. Practices "make sense" because they align or extend out of normative logic formations, engaged as a matter of course. Through their appeal to common sense, such practices most often remain invisible; they escape notice because they remain unquestioned—they extend the norms that make them possible. As a consequence, it is the role of materialist inquiry to disrupt such normative processes—to make strange the familiar.

As more contemporary theorists have pointed out (Certeau, Deleuze, Foucault, etc.), once practices are divorced from their material contexts, they exist as mere representations, closing off possibility for change as they order matter in particular ways. This led quite rightly to scholars recognizing the "crisis of representation" within research. Importantly, this research crisis is two-fold. Firstly, representations of some reality always fall short—they can never fully define or otherwise account for the reality they seek to represent (they always exist as representations of, never the reality itself). This is a *crisis of descriptive failure* and has been discussed in numerous research texts. Secondly, the crisis of representation stems from an inability for inquiry to act on (or within) anything but the representations it creates. This is a *crisis of engagement* and is less acknowledged in the literature. Indeed, it is this second failure—that we can only knowledgably encounter and change that which we create (representations)—that raises inevitable questions about the material impact of our work and concerns regarding the viability of social justice inquiry. Situating inquiry as ensconced in representationalism limits the goals and impacts of inquiry in the name of social change. As such, refusing the representationalist trap in favor of an integrated, dynamic, intrarelation among matter and practices raises specific activist-oriented questions: How can we impact matter in order to create the possibility for new practices?

As such, it is perhaps the first step for materialist inquiry to make incompletely visible that which it seeks to analyze (a process that Foucault [1998] termed "problematization"). This peripheral visibility (always extending beyond the edges of our vision) makes possible critical alternatives—ways of knowing and being—that would otherwise remain unrecognized. This is inquiry as a productive force—as exceeding itself and the very rationalities that grant it its initial theoretical traction.[5] Refusing the easy bifurcation of the ontic and epistemic means that new ways of knowing are simultaneously met by new ways of being—new practices are made possible, extending from the very excess of nontraditional logic formations. Thus it is that practices carry with them the logic that makes them possible. Importantly, practices are contextually situated and fully material—there are no extramaterial practices. As such, the close examination of social practices calls forth principles of materialism—more specifically, the new materialism that extends from process-based thinking.

As an example of the productive use of problematization, consider Davies's (2010) interrogation of the *neoliberal subject* in order to provoke alternative renderings and newly arrived-at inquiry practices. In juxtaposition to the traditionally fixed subject that is inevitably limited within the neoliberal rationale (what St. Pierre termed the *humanist subject*), Davies asks qualitative researchers to "[think] the subject differently" in an attempt to locate "the subject" as a sociohistorical entity—"both an idea *and* an accomplishment that we labour over" (55). Through locating the neoliberal subject as a concept that we strive to attain (and, of course, can never fully achieve), Davies asks critical inquirers to then consider the conditions of possibility through which "the subject is (and should be) … and with what effect" (55). Along these lines, Davies goes on to ask three key questions, all bent on interrogating the neoliberal subject and thereby making space for alternative manifestations of being (alternative ontological possibilities):

> How is one kind of subjecthood or another made possible? How does one set of possibilities become normalized such that the subject cannot imagine itself otherwise? And most important, how can the human subject evolve beyond the current sets of actions and reactions? (55)

In this sense Davies's questions point to the productive possibility of being otherwise, of agency not as a commodified product (that one has or hopes to purchase) but rather as "*conditions of possibility*" (55, original emphasis)—the ambiguity of the future in which the subject has not fully formed. This is the subject not as a full representation but as existing on the periphery of what is known and assumptions about what might be.

Importantly this shift from considerations regarding what-has-become to the future possibilities inherent in what-is-yet-to-become changes how we think about ethics, risk, and responsibility. Whereas the traditional neoliberal subject calls forth an *ethic of achievement* (have you achieved the ideal of neoliberal individuality, of economically productive citizenry?), more poststructural ethics emphasize a *material immanence,* one that links all forms of life through relational forms of being (in what ways do our practices resist foreclosure, opening new possibilities not yet defined?). A stance of necessarily peripheral ethical engagement.

Obviously this shift affects thoughts regarding our ethical approaches to methodological practice. Ethical alignments with neoliberal rationales emphasize the importance of producing closed subjects, with unitary voices, distinct and recognizable from the contexts from which they emerge. More poststructural approaches to methodology would instead look for the ambiguities inherent in relation—spaces and interstices where individuals blur into the material conditions of their existence. Here, as Davies (2010) notes, agency is "linked to the opening up of new ways of being" (56).

As Davies shows, neoliberalism is not simply a theoretical description of abstract principles and practices. As an always-emergent political rationality, neoliberalism asserts itself at a material level, producing affective responses and states that are, in turn, incorporated into contemporary subjectivities. As Cole (2011) frames it, there is a "living out" of neoliberal values that "stays with the population" as they come to take on, transform, and re-articulate a series of manufactured values and beliefs (9). As such, Cole goes on to note the importance of methodologically mapping out social cartographies to show the "ways in which society is changing under the influence of accelerated post-modern capitalism" (9). For Cole, this mapping-out is very much a materialist endeavor.

As a means for engaging in materialist methodological work, Cole (2011) advocates for an "affective research strategy" that "treats all data as a form of becoming" (12). In this scenario the methodologist does not seek to solely unravel some entwined bundle of meaning—seeking clarity from otherwise over-layered forms of data—but instead prods the affective assemblages of being, maintaining the contradictions and blurred connections of being without normalizing their meaning. This is to say that the materialist methodologist foregoes the façade of clarity (Pasque et al. 2012) that comes from normative data analysis—a practice built upon the *logic of extraction* and representational assumptions—in favor of a becoming form of analysis that remains open, invoking new meanings and ways of being instead of claiming the deadened, closed figures of meaning-made.

Consider also Wanda Pillow's (2003) useful methodological approach of feminist genealogy as a means to "shift the gaze of inquiry" from the pregnant girls who participated in her study to "the discourses shaping and defining teen pregnancy, without losing the contexts of the girls' lived experiences" (148). In this way Pillow refuses a methodological fixation on the girls and their confected/isolated identities (as pregnant, as teens, as pregnant teens) in favor of the very discourses that make such identities and constructions possible. Pillow invokes a genealogical analysis that is suspicious of truth claims based on assumed rationality, and she "disputes understandings of subjects as singular, easily identifiable, linear subjects" (150). Following a decidedly Foucualdian approach to materialism, Pillow's is an example of how rational logics and normative subject formation might be necessarily decentered and refused. Consequently, the constructed subject is not the focus of such inquiry but rather the constructing-of-the-subject—the means by which such subjects come to be, are understood, and interpreted. Through this approach, the fixation on the subject is made "irrational"—that which allows the coming-to-sense is questioned to the extent that prefabricated sense and sense-making is no longer easy; commonsense fails. Through specifically challenging fundamental values of enlightenment—of rationality as natural, of science as neutral, of both as moving us progressively toward some possible truth—the discourses surrounding teen pregnancy are productively interrogated and (re)considered. Thus, Pillow's project remains more fluid than not—refusing isolated identities and extracted ways of knowing, she allows methodological approaches, lived practices, and indeterminate interpretation to overflow and bleed into one another, causing her to claim the valuable possibilities inherent in the "interruptive excessiveness of bodies and theory" (148). As excessive, "bodies and theory" cannot be contained, nor may they be fully represented. This recognition of the excessive circumstance in which representation inevitably fails calls to mind the goals and inquiry practices found in Desjarlais's and Wacquant's work surveyed earlier; they remain linked through a materialist orientation to inquiry, one that refuses the extractive logics of the status quo. Like these other materialist scholars, Pillow's inquiry approach allows for a critique of common sense—historically produced patterns of knowing and coming to know, exposing "the power of the norm" (149).

Importantly, the productive alternatives made possible through the critical inquiry of scholars such as Cole, Davies, and Pillow remain materially situated. This is to say that emphasizing onto-epistemological visions of change simultaneously foregrounds that all change is material change—there is no sense of "pure discourse" that remains divorced from material context. This is the basis of the materialism I put forth throughout this book. When considering such issues as methodological responsibility, ethics, work, and practice, I am most interested in the material connections of such terms. I remain uninterested in theoretical orientations that bifurcate the material from the discursive. Hence, mine is an interest in what I term *materialist methodologies*—those inquiry approaches that recognize the productive impact of materiality in coming to know and coming to be—an onto-epistemological materiality. As an example, Foucault's (2003) analysis of the movement from a disciplinary to a regulatory society might be read as a similar decentering of the subject that takes on the import of social justice and emphasizes the social implications of a materialist approach to research. Foucault (2003) recognizes the intersections of micro- and macro-practices evident in techniques of power and the right to kill. He writes, "When I say 'killing,' I obviously do not mean simply murder as such, but also every form of indirect murder: the fact of exposing someone to death, increasing the risk of death for some people, or, quite simply, political death, expulsion, rejection, and so on." (256) Language derives from material experiences and has material effects. With respect to subjectivity, the discursive structures that privilege certain identities over others also enclose particular bodies, and these enclosures convey the right to live and the right to let die.

Yet it remains important to recognize that this orientation toward the productively relational quality of materialism is not entirely new (in the contemporary sense); it has historical roots that cannot be ignored. As Papadopoulos (2010) notes, there remains an important connection between Marx's early work on materialism and more contemporary neomaterialist scholarship—both emphasize "matter as a vital force" (66). In Papadopoulos's reading of Marx, materialism necessarily connotes an "activist dimension" in which multiple materialist forms (inorganic matter, everyday social life, biological matter) collude toward "the collective capacity to affect material change" (66). In this sense materiality cannot be separated from (social, political, daily) practices; the two cannot be conceptualized independent from one another. As a consequence, Papadopoulos asserts, "Materialism without activism is not transformative, in fact it is impossible" (67). In this way Marx offers us a glimpse of an *activist materialism*, one that refuses to separate materiality from social practices and possibilities for material transformation. I submit that a materialist approach to inquiry necessarily maintains this "activist dimension," thereby necessitating alterations to how we come to consider and engage issues of *responsibility* and *risk* as elements of methodological practice.

Whereas up to this point I have emphasized a materialist orientation toward knowing and being that is relational in order, leading to processual forms of inquiry that begin with the notion of *problematization*, new materialism shifts the orientation of this relation: more than the notion of relationality between or among entities, there exist only relations within. Thus, the new materialist perspective does away with atomistic thinking—that there are isolatable elements that exist independent of one another—in favor of meaning-making as a congruent event. The result of such newly materialist perspectives is the promise of inquiry-as-intervention and the challenge of establishing an ethical orientation that guides research practices for social justice.

On Critical (New) Materialism

In the following overview of new materialism my aim is not to provide a comprehensive articulation of a complex (and rather diverse) theoretical framework. Mine is not an attempt to capture or otherwise render the totality of a new materialist paradigm. Indeed, striving to discern all of the dynamic differences in approaches to new materialism is akin to attempting to explicate all of the elements, approaches, traditions, and practices of Marxism—the attempt inevitably falls short (and, of course, is not theoretically congruent with materialist approaches that foreground the overdetermination of concepts and the like). And yet there should be some overarching assumptions about how we live, know, and come to know that draw together select approaches under the umbrella of Marxism or new materialism respectively (with the understanding, in true materialist form, that such paradigmatic boundaries are never fixed nor fully developed).

Instead, I want to point out how the recent embrace of new materialism in some circles presents methodological possibilities that cannot be ignored. As a consequence, what follows is a consideration for how a new materialist orientation toward inquiry offers otherwise overlooked possibilities for making meaning. Further, the overarching assumptions that help to define new materialism both align with and provoke the *parrhesiastic* approach to truth-telling that is the basis for the next chapter. In short, new materialism offers productive ontological, epistemological, and ethical assumptions that give nuance to the materially oriented approach of *parrhesia*. It is my view that the worldviews asserted by new materialism make possible an integration of *parrhesia* that Foucault perhaps thought not possible. As Foucault (2001) has noted, *parrhesia* cannot exist in a world ruled by Cartesian duality; instead, we need differently materialist epistemological assumptions of the world. Perhaps new materialism offers us a productive entré into this difference, thereby making space for *parrhesia* as all the more relevant (and necessary) to our contemporary contexts.

Though like all arrangements of thought, new materialists certainly encompass a variety of perspectives and approaches; they are most alike in their determination that linguistic or textual accounts of being fall short of their explanatory goals. More directly, traditional approaches to inquiry are shown to never fully consider the dynamic relations of meaning and matter—that is, how matter itself has an agential role in the creation of meaning. According to new materialist thought, matter is active, fluid, and productive. As a consequence, those inquiry practices that fixate on meaning-making as a fully human endeavor miss the multiple ways in which matter itself affects the world. Traditional inquiry practices might thus be shown as overly anthropocentric, furthering the unnecessary separation between humans and nonhumans, social and material, culture and nature.

To begin, we need to address how new or critical materialism understands the notion of matter. Contrary to post/positivistic conceptions of matter—those that relied upon the easy separation of mind and matter—contemporary approaches emphasize the indeterminacy of matter as well as its productivity and resilience (Coole and Frost 2010). Far from a defined "thing," matter remains unformed, in continuous variation (Papadopoulos 2010). In this sense the turn toward matter (making *matter* matter, as Barad [2003] would have it) is an opening up, materiality as possibility. As Coole and Frost (2010) write, "materiality is always something more than 'mere' matter: an excess, force, vitality, relationality, or difference that renders matter active, self-creative, productive, unpredictable" (9). As the authors go on to note, new materialists share the assertion that, "'matter becomes' rather than that 'matter is'" (10). Becoming matter aligns with the ever-unfinished relational materiality described earlier.

This reconsideration of the productive possibilities inherent in matter has significant implications for those of us who take inquiry seriously. The basic tenets of critical geography recognize the material world as an active contributor to processes of meaning-making—material contexts can no longer be read to simply "contain" meaning or serve as an empty backdrop against which meaning is played. Further, critical geographers insist that the material world is historical, imbued with a host of sociopolitical meanings and values that shift and change with time and perspective. As a result, the material world is never closed or fixed; it remains open to new contexts and meanings even as it has a developing hand in the production of such contexts and meanings. A new or critical materialist perspective pushes the perspective of critical geography even further through asserting a becoming matter that is decidedly more active and productively unpredictable than previously claimed by critical geographers. Matter is always excessive, always becoming more than what is—or could be—known. This recognition of matter's excess aligns well with the articulation of intervention, noted earlier in this chapter. As a consequence, matter, in all its open excess, might exemplify important interventions into the normative status quo. This is matter as disruptive intervention into traditionally bound patterns of meaning-making.

Take as an example the limited means by which traditional methodologies pay cursory attention to matter as some general form of context. In this scenario context might offer a rationale for rendering meaning in some particular way. Context provides closure of meaning, a way to justify the particularity of interpretation. Matter is thus situated as a material backdrop to the formation of context. Examples in this sense might include the physical "context" of an inner-city school or even a table consisting of demographic information of participants. Traditional methodological approaches might understand these as contexts that *place* the study (in the inner city) or *group* the participants (as gendered, raced, even aged in particularly developmental contexts). Here context is a descriptive backdrop that, at the same time, binds the study—context as closure.

A new materialist perspective, however, situates matter more agentially, working against closure and toward a becoming possibility that is both ontological and epistemological in order. In this sense material context does not simply provide the particular nuances through which select claims might be made; rather, matter remains endlessly generative, always exceeding the net of "context" cast upon it. As Coole and Frost (2010) write, a new materialist perspective insists "upon the openness, contingency, unevenness, and complexity of materialization as an ongoing process within which social actors and theorists are irremediably immersed" (28). In this sense new materialists offer matter as a productive force, one we would do well to recognize and attend to in our projects for social change. To extend the earlier example, an "inner-city" or "urban" school now implies meanings that exceed their assumed categorization. The actual material school itself makes possible select student practices all the while constraining others. To not be a delinquent student, one must perhaps cross the material threshold of the school, moving through the built landscape, embodying the role of the *good* student. Here, the urban geography intersects with the sociohistorical identity process, calling to the fore concomitant practices of knowing and being that can never be fully captured unto themselves. The geographic landscape becomes part-and-parcel with the event of schooling in that moment—an event never fully predicted, open to possibilities for change. This is an engagement in the immediate, not a methodological capture of the past.

Principles of new materialism offer a relational view of knowing/being and, as a consequence, differently conceptualize inquiry in the name of social justice. In this scenario, efforts are made to follow the threads of entanglement, the multiple relations that make up constellations of meaning. This entails a *flattening* of onto-epistemological models and fully relational intersections of being. Often such work entails interrogating contradictions that manifest throughout these relations as well as the daily practices through which such contradictions are obscured. Deleuze and Guattari (1972) talked about this as schizo-analysis. For example, instead of trying to liberate voice (an instance of extrativist methodologies interrogated in the previous chapter), a new materialist approach might detail the event of voice, the multiple intersecting planes of being out of which voice stems. Here voice is not a thing, not a commodity to be passed through the academic market, but is instead made possible by an endless array of processes and corresponding practices that *are* context. Voice thus remains thoroughly material (voice can no longer be fully metaphorical, extending as it does through the physiological intra-action of breath with sound with embodied movement) even as it intersects with the sociopolitical discourse of our times. The key here might be to recognize what is said (previously, voice) as more than repetition—as *difference.*

For Deleuze (1995) difference is not negative but productive: difference is thinking. The goal, then, is to deterritorialize voice, to make it lack sense, with the hope of becoming differently. One might do so by interrogating the intra-active properties that make voice possible. The question shifts from "Where is voice and how can it be returned?" (a question of liberation through location) to "How does voice work? What intra-actions are made possible through the production of voice?" Voice here might be shown as distributed, an enacted relation of being/becoming that is decidedly material. In this sense thematic representations of voice (the consensus of voice) give way to what Barad (2007) terms a *diffractive reading* of patterned difference. Voice is thus known within its entangled meaning. The materialist methodologist might thus seek to engage voice as an emergent process "within which more or less enduring structures and assemblages sediment and congeal, sometimes as a result of their internal inertia but also as a manifestation of the powerful interests invested therein" (Coole and Frost 2010, 29)—voice as distinctly material and political inquiry as the means through which to productively disrupt the sociopolitical sedimentation of voice in normative ways.

As an example, Pearce and MacLure's (2009) methodological work emphasizes a refusal to allow the present, situated, and identified position to dominate their inquiry project. Instead, the authors ask "how absence and differences rather than presence and consensus might be worked through, traversed and unfolded" (250). In many ways a focus on "absence and differences" decenters the traditional allegiance to fixed presence in productive ways and is akin to my own earlier request to consider the peripheral in our inquiry projects (Kuntz and Presnall 2012). Yet it remains important to recognize that theirs is a methodological orientation toward the unknown that is strikingly distinct from traditional fixations on difference-as-deviance. Further, explorations of "absence and differences rather than presence and consensus" provide a different type of unfolding with particular implications for how the methodological community has engaged with the notion of voice.

Consider in this instance the role of silence. All too often silence is considered the absence of meaning, a gap in the formation of meaning-making. When I work with students who are new to interviewing or focus groups, for example, I often ask why we are so quick to fill the silences of our interactions—as though silence pointed to some mistake, for example, a poorly formed interview question, a misunderstanding, or some type of discomfort. Silence, in this instance, stands in for lack (at times silence is even understood as nearly the opposite of voice—one is "silenced," voice is removed from possibility). Similarly, throughout the educational arena silence is often interpreted as a lack of knowing. Consider the ease with which rapidity of response is mistaken for intelligence/knowing in K–16 classrooms. Traditionally a question is asked, and there is a race among students to answer. (The intensity of physical response to knowing seems rather consistently aligned with student age—elementary students often leap out of their chairs with their quick responses; high school students less so. By the time students make their way through college they seem decidedly less interested in making their quick responses known or visible in the classroom.) In this instance we would do well to recognize that thoughtful responses take time; silence need not be aligned with a lack of knowledge or disinterestedness in the classroom or even the research site. Of course, it need not always be this way, particularly if we are to read silence relationally. As Sharpe (2014) notes, "Silence can be a way of not becoming a slave to one's actions and self-representations, of not being captured by them in the fantasy of a consistent subjectivity" (38). Again, silence in this sense might be a disruption to the momentum of the normative, a creative means for making possible new meaning. Far from a lack of meaning or an absence of sense, silence here is excess, disrupting normative claims on meaning through resisting foreclosure or complete definition—silence as a becoming resistance.

Finally, an important contribution of new materialism extends from a useful collapse of ways of being with ways of knowing with an ethical positioning against closure. This exists as an extension of the relational perspective of new materialism and is perhaps best exemplified in the work of Karen Barad. In response to the glorification of the humanist subject detailed in Chapter 2, Barad

(2007) offers a relational, posthumanist ontology that "refuses the representationalist fixation on 'words' and 'things'" (132). Inherent in this posthumanist ontology is a *"relationship between specific exclusionary practices embodied as specific material configurations of the world* (i.e., discursive practices/(con) figurations rather than 'words') *and specific material phenomena* (i.e., relations rather than 'things')" (132; original emphasis). As such, Barad's relational way of knowing and coming to know reveals normalized processes as well as those logics of extraction that separate "things" from their relations. This is sustained inquiry as an intervention into habitualized formations of being. Relationally speaking, Barad is interested in traditional formations of *coming to sense*—a materially embedded and incessantly relational process—rather than simply *what makes sense.*

In counter-distinction to the Cartesian cut that affects meaning for extractivist logics, Barad (2007) offers what she terms an "agential cut" (133) between subjects and objects. The *agential cut* makes meaning possible within relations, not in addition to them. As such, Barad emphasizes a distinction between intra-action and inter-action. As a prefix, *intra* means "within," whereas *inter* designates "between." Though at first glance this distinction may seem trivial, it does recognize an important shift in how we philosophically consider the production of meaning in our posthumanist times. Generally speaking, to conceive of relations "between" two or more entities is to assume their preexistence before their relation (that is, that they were discrete and contained things before entering into relation). Meaning is thus generated through the coming together of two already-formed entities within some preexistent context. This is an intersection of entities that have their own histories and conditions unto themselves; they exist fully *prior* to their relation. Beginning from the notion of "intra," however, recognizes that the relations themselves are constitutive and never absent their material contexts. More simply, *inter*-relations align with traditional Cartesian thinking that distinguishes between subjects and objects prior to (or external to) phenomena. *Intra*-relations, however, do not allow for preexisting relations but rather emphasize emergent relations within phenomena. Consequently, traditional conceptions of causality no longer find logical traction within Barad's relational model. As Coole and Frost (2010) write, "there is no longer a quantitative relationship between cause and effect" the result of which means that "it is impossible either to predict outcomes in advance or to repeat an event" (14). Methodologically speaking, this loss of prediction and repetition is productive indeed.

Further still, Barad's insistence on intra-relations shifts the notion of self-other that has dominated the field of inquiry since the *crisis of representation* and productively alters what one risks to tell the truth, *parrhesiastically* speaking. To be "in relation" is to be within, not without—among, not between. Truth-telling risks that relation within, thus simultaneously risking one's identity (who one is in that relation), citizenship (a recognized self within the community), and reality (one's dynamic relation to the world in which we live). This is an ontologically charged relation to inquiry. In challenging the other, one challenges the self (hence the dynamic and material sense of relation). This newly formed relation among identity, citizenship, and reality is a key element of my discussion of *parrhesiastic* inquiry for social justice, explicated in Chapter 4. Barad's work with new materialism opens the door for truth-telling in the name of materialist social justice—what I locate as a contemporary practice of *parrhesia*. Such relations importantly challenge traditional practices of methodological responsibility.

As Pearce and MacLure (2009) note, "Questions of who we are, and what our relations to others might be, involve a rethinking of responsibility" (250). In this way questions of identity (who we are) and our relationality (our relations to others) necessarily question normative claims regarding responsibility; as soon as we question who we are and how we relate, we necessarily rethink our ties toward our selves, others, and the very relations through which we are known. As Barad (2012) articulates, "Responsibility is not an obligation that the subject chooses, but rather an incarnate relation that precedes the intentionality of consciousness. Responsibility is not a calculation to be performed. It is a relation ... an iterative (re)opening up to, an enabling responsiveness" (34). In responsibility therein lies questions of response—the ability to respond to contexts and circumstances in particular ways. Further, as Pearce and MacLure make clear, this "response-ability" necessarily stems from the possibility to engage with the unknown, an openness to indeterminacy that "we need to have in order to welcome the unknown and avoid responding in our habitual, unthinking ways" (250). As a consequence, responsibility is given new dimensionality as an ethical orientation toward refusing habitual, common-sensical responses that stem from normative rationalities. Considerations of methodological responsibility, in this rethinking, must extend beyond procedural ethics to the very ability to encounter and relate within unknown ways of knowing and coming to know—an epistemological and ontologically oriented place of indeterminacy. Further, as Bennett (2010) notes, an insistence on the intrarelation between humans and things (the vibrancy of matter) "presents individuals as simply incapable of bearing *full* responsibility for their effects" (37, original emphasis). In this sense responsibility is always partial—never particular—and we must thus shift our relation to the ethical. There is no one source for blame, no absolute claim for who or what is responsible for particular effects/impacts. Thus, instead of looking for some subject to bear (or claim) *full* responsibility, we must instead foreground ethical deliberations on those material relations through which we come to be. Ours is thus an ethical imperative to inquiry differently, to refuse the constraint of the status quo.

In the end Barad (2007) points to the overlap of knowing and being with important consequences for our work in qualitative inquiry: "Practices of knowing and being are not isolable: they are materially implicated. We don't obtain knowledge by standing outside the world; we know because we are *of* the world" (185, original emphasis). Barad's assertion of the inseparability of knowing and being stems from a refusal to dwell in traditionally assumed binaries: "human and nonhuman, subject and object, mind and body, matter and discourse" (185). This turn to understand phenomena as constructions within relations leads Barad to a sense of ethico-onto-epistemology: "the intertwining of ethics, knowing, and being" (185). (Keep in mind this infusion of ethical, ontic, and epistemic concerns as exemplified by the new materialist orientation when we encounter Foucault's presentation of truth-telling as *parrhesia* in Chapter 4.)

Not to be dismissed is the more subtle shift from dialectical to more dialogic means of relation that accompanies the materialist transfer into new materialism. Both dialectical and dialogical orientations toward inquiry emphasize relational meaning-making that is fully material and demonstrate an antagonism to oppositional thinking. And due to assumptions of relationality, both approaches begin from epistemological assertions of fluidity (over fixity) and movement (over stasis). However, it is the means by which dialectic and dialogic approaches engage with the inevitable production of contradiction and/or dissonance that differentiates them, with rather important implications for inquiry.

As a gloss—dialectical approaches recognize a relational difference within processes that result in inevitable contradictions and shortfalls. What is interesting to dialectical approaches are the means by which such contradictions are accounted for or otherwise resolved. Hence there is a tendency toward compromise or some other resolution out of conflict and contradiction. Some might argue that dialectical approaches to inquiry thus inevitably conclude with some sort of synthesis, a merging of contradiction that dulls the distinctions that mark difference. For many social critics, then, dialectical approaches to inquiry are necessarily reductionist (bound as they are to the integration, resolution, or synthesis—choose your merging metaphor—of difference/contradiction).

Like dialecticism, dialogical forms of meaning-making locate contradictions as extending from an endless series of materially situated relations. From a dialogic approach, however, those contradictions are never resolved—they impact and make possible new performances of difference—the diffractive practices of meaning-making that are a hallmark of new materialism. As a consequence, whereas dialectical approaches move toward resolution, more dialogic orientations toward inquiry emphasize an opening up of meaning, the production of more meaning-full relations. This is a becoming-meaning, one that could never be resolved nor synthesized. This opening up of meaning aligns well with Barad's notion of constructing a "diffractive reading," wherein the critical inquirer experiments with patterns of relationality to recognize how they might shift and change with each new opening up of relational meaning. This materialist work, as Barad (2012) notes, is not about "synthesizing different points of view from the outside" (as dialectical reasoning might have it) "but rather about ... putting 'oneself' at risk" (34). Diffractive reading, then, extends toward the risky possibility of being otherwise, yet doing so through becoming differently within the very phenomena one might claim to study.

Wandering Toward Methodological Naïveté

Given the disruptive relational perspective offered by new critical materialism, how might we revise our methodological orientations to affect a progressive sense of social change? Perhaps we begin with an openness to seem method-ologically naïve, to openly resist the reductive critique of realism. This might begin with shifting our collective focus to engage with that which is not fully in our frame of reference—an ethic of peripheral knowing.

In her examination of vibrant matter, Bennett (2010) claims a method-ological "willingness to appear naive or foolish" (xiii). Following Bennett (and others), we might ask what it means to be methodologically naïve, to operate from a place of less-than-certainty, an openness to new and unexpected ways of knowing and coming to know. Perhaps this methodological naïveté intersects with my reading of Certeau's notion of wandering, examined in the previous chapter. How might we naïvely wander the methodological landscape? To na-ïvely encounter the world is to refuse the binds of formal training, unaffected by the bonds of historical rationalities. Deleuze (1990) considered "naïve philosophy" the "most innocent" and thus feels the least guilt about engaging in rawly material analysis (88–89). As Bennett succinctly states, "There is thus something to be said for moments of methodological naiveté" (17). In what might be seen as a call for more radical methodological innovation—innovative practices that extend from an engaged ontologically based materiality—Ben-nett (2010) asks that we "devise new procedures, technologies, and regimes of perception" that make possible alternative ways of knowing, coming to know, and living (108).

In my view, this is to lay claim to an emergent ontological view, one that carries with it an ethics of the peripheral. To be peripheral is to never be fully known—our peripheral vision only gives a fleeting sense of location and definition. As Braidotti (2002) notes, "nothing happens at the centre, for Deleuze, but at the periphery, there roam the youthful gangs of the new nomads" (78). To engage the peripheral is to articulate what is there even with the recognition that the glimpse is fleeting. The movement of the peripheral—the playful way in which it resists the fixed stare—is thus not cause to refuse a truth-telling; it is rather an opportunity to make visible relational truths-in-movement, truth without a predetermined end.

This is a critically materialist truth-telling, one that does not align the articulation of truth with fabricated certainty. It is also an ethical decision to engage in the political fray—to locate the past and future in the present moment of truth-telling. Similarly, Denzin and Giardina (2014) point to the transformative possibilities of such critical work: "As critical scholars, our task is to make history present, to make the future present, to undo the past" (18). In order to simultaneously address historicized misreadings of the past even as we actively imagine a more socially just future, we need the capacity to think differently, to unhinge ourselves from legitimated knowledge formations. In very real ways this is to "undo the past"—it is a determination to simultaneously be other than we are and other than we have been. It is a naïve engagement with the periphery. In order to link such an ethical orientation toward inquiry with daily practices, I turn next to a further examination of *parrhesia*.

Chapter 4

Methodological Parrhesia: *Truth-Telling*

Introduction

I begin this chapter by noting the many ways in which the inherent contradictions of our contemporary moment require a sustained materialist critique, one that foregrounds considerations of truth and an ethic of responsible risk, through which new practices of being might be enacted toward the realization of progressive social change. In this way I more directly consider the realities of a globalized neoliberalism (interrogated in Chapter 2) against the critically relational perspective of critical or new materialism (discussed in Chapter 3). I then link our contemporary materialist moment (of disorientation, of a challenging collapse between truth and fiction) with a shift in conceptions of power from enacted on and through bodies to a more affective governing at the level of population (a dynamic transition that Foucault characterizes as one from disciplinary power to biopower). Through these connections I seek in this chapter to show how an engaged materialist practice of philosophical *parrhesia* usefully intervenes within contemporary ontological and epistemological formations through a practiced ethic of truth-telling and sustained risk of the very identities/subjectivities through which we are known. More simply put, a *parrhesiastic* approach to inquiry engages in social justice work through risky

The Responsible Methodologist: Inquiry, Truth-Telling, and Social Justice, by Aaron M. Kuntz, 93–120.

practices of truth-telling—this is inquiry in the name of a political project for progressive change.

Social Schizophrenia: The Problem of Social Truths

I am often struck by the profound contradictions that are the fabric of our daily lives. We recognize as rational that we must maintain peace by waging war, take on debt to improve economic viability, and improve standardized tests to more efficiently capture creative thinking. More than Orwellian *doublethink,* there exists today a simultaneity of contrary truths that collude to produce an affective state of disorientation and apathetic distance. Most often such circumstances are driven by a collapse of micro- and macro-perspectives that are made to coexist through a circumspect system of logic and often contradictory practices. Critical geographers term this a collapse of scale and link its impact to the ongoing processes of a globalized neoliberalism.

As an extended example, consider the strange hold that economic health has on us today. One of the more anxiety-inducing "markers" of economic health is the credit score. It has become relatively common knowledge that in order to achieve a strong credit score, one needs to take on debt (i.e., obtain and use a credit card and/or a house mortgage) and show that one can manage financially while in debt. The inability to adequately manage debt is noted in one's credit score and negatively affects future buying power and more (some employers have reportedly begun using credit scores to evaluate job applicants). Further still, credit scores have been linked to identities—who we are as people (e.g., whether we have "good sense" or are fiscally irresponsible). Although the impact of our credit scores might be felt on the individual level, they also play out on the national level, generating comparative points of data across populations. Indeed, there are a host of online articles and advertisements all seeking to help individuals improve their credit scores through invoking a series of legitimated practices, even attitudes, in relation to "proper" economic functioning. Such espoused practices aim to remedy poor credit scores regardless of immediate locale—when read against the neoliberal norms of academic determinacy, immediate context loses its explanatory power.

Perhaps more than the actual contextual contradictions of our lives, I am struck by the amount of energy and time that goes into managing (or rationalizing away) such contradictions. These are the actual daily practices that might usefully be the objects of our critical inquiry. Though certainly coming to grips with our contradictory lives has been an ongoing practice for some time (and, some might say, a condition of postmodernity[1]), there is increasing concern for the ways in which such incongruities work to instill collective affective states—of disorientation, paralysis, or even bemusement. Of course, this recognition of contradiction is not new—Marx's dialectical approach, for example, has certainly inspired a whole multitude of analyses of social contradictions in numerous fields over time. However, unlike attempts to resolve contradictions through synthesis—as the dialectical approach might have it—our contemporary moment entails allowing such contradictions to remain side-by-side, distinct, and without full resolution. Because of this, our unique time of nonresolution makes possible the formation of a whole host of deeply felt social anxieties. These affective states of being develop within a complementary overproduction of often contradictory truths and an inability (and/or collective disinterestedness) to differentiate truth from falsity.

Importantly, these contradictions often flow from a disorienting overproduction of truths that are generated absent a materialist basis for context; they exist through their extraction. As such, negotiating these times and spaces of incongruent meaning requires a collective effort, one that takes place at the level of the social (or what Foucault [2007, 2008] came to term the level of population) and is simultaneously enacted at the level of the local. In this way the inherent challenges of globalized neoliberalism require a sustained response that simultaneously brings together individual activity and social practices of meaning-making. This is a collective means of "making sense" and often develops as a way to gloss over—though never overcome—shared experiences of ontological contradiction. Perhaps newly critical analyses are necessary.

Of course, research practices of all kinds are a significant means by which such social contradictions are managed—traditionally, research has been the avenue for making sense, for producing "sensible" insights, where previously there had been but ambiguity. In this case, traditional research works to manage or justify gaps in meaning-making, interstices in the otherwise unbroken production of common sense. Yet, as alluded to throughout this book, traditional research does not overcome the many deficits and problematics inherent in logics of extraction; indeed, it depends on them for visibility and extends their common status through their employment. Further, traditional mechanisms for making-meaning (and the logics that inform them) are themselves culpable in an overproduction of extracted truths, leading to an affective state of disorientation that has come to dominate our contemporary moment. As such, any inquiry process that seeks to intervene in traditional formations of knowing and being—that is, any project that is engaged with the hope for social justice and progressive change—must necessarily grapple with the means by which truth is produced and sustained in our culture.

Returning to the example of credit scores for a moment, one might recognize the ease with which credit scores contribute to what Ben Baez (2014) terms the "data-basing of our lives." The database (and those techniques that populate the database with quantified data) makes possible the comparison of multiple data points at the level of population, broadening the relational possibilities through which we are made visible or known. The credit score pulls in a host of economic data that are then set against a generated series of statistical norms—the square by which "healthy" economic function is known. These normed data are then brought to bear back on the individual, defining him/her in terms of economic value and even prescribing future activities (such as those practices aimed at repairing deviant credit scores, alluded to earlier). In this sense credit scores have achieved a level of "truth" within contemporary society, one that defines us as well as enables and constrains select activities. Thus, such truths pull from the level of population in order to act upon the individual

Once made visible—in this case, given a credit score—the individual may thus enhance or alter economic activity accordingly; the disciplined body generates new actions, new ways of being, in response to remaining statistically visible in particular ways. Critically the only way to "speak back" to one's visibility is to take on legitimated practices and make them one's own. There is no challenging the rationality of the system or the statistical values that drive its production; instead, one can act differently, more in line with economic norms—that is, one can discipline oneself to the values of the market. This has entirely material significance: one feels the anxiety of being statistically known (the vulnerability that comes with such visibility), even as one engages in material practices to "correct" that self-knowledge. Select "truths," developed at the intersection of statistically rendered population and individual daily practice, inform one's affective state, granting a decidedly material legitimacy to statistical knowledge formations. There are no means to resolve any contradictions in this flow from population to individual and back again—one must simply maintain their co-existence, acting in relation to their ongoing production. The result is a reality of contradictions that borders on the absurd.[2]

Further still, this movement toward population-level recognition results in select affective states that encourage a type of social docility. This is not simply the charge of political apathy or laziness that older generations lob at, say, millennials; instead, this manifests as a collectively felt sense of fear made most visible during national security emergencies or socio-environmental tragedies such as

Hurricane Katrina or the Tuscaloosa tornado of 2011 (Kuntz 2015). The result of such shared affective states is a re-emphasis on *security* as the political trump card—we give ourselves over to manufactured protections against risk. This manifests, of course, in individual practices (paying agencies to monitor credit scores, sending our children to private schools, installing home security devices) and larger social norms (recognizing the need for governments to read/interpret our data—be they e-mail or cell phone records, even what books we order from Amazon). No longer (just) the individual docile body (as in Foucault's disciplinary power formations), these collective affective states develop a normalized docility at the level of population. In this way manifestations of biopower link the individual with the collective through *affect*; developed practices aim to maintain a visibility within a culture of the dividual—the conversion of people into data (see Chapter 2). Through the incessant production of the dividual, there develops a collective resignation—truth-telling seems lost in a sea of contradiction.

In his keynote address to the 2014 Deleuzian Studies Conference, Ian Buchanan noted that ours is a time of absurdity, when falsity and truth are displayed side-by-side with equal standing. This stems from the notion that we "know" multiple truths and yet have no sufficient means to act in direct relation to them, resulting in a schizo-society that is paralyzed by its inability to differentiate among an ever-growing availability of truth claims. As Buchanan (2014) went on to assert, schizophrenia thus exists as a social illness that recognizes more truths than one can possibly act upon; the real and unreal collude to disorient the schizoid into nonaction. Given the layered perversity of globalized neoliberalism, schizophrenia is not a metaphorical description of our times; we literally live within a schizo-society. As a result, exposing what is not true (what is false) is no longer a means toward changing the system in any revolutionary way (as the critical theorists of old, perhaps, had it). It is not the production of falsehoods that is the contemporary problem; it is the incessant production of multiple and often contradictory truths that lead to our schizophrenic state (Buchanan 2014). Perhaps this is why "critical" scholarship has lost its disruptive edge—*calling attention to falsehoods fails the schizo-society.* Instead, it is the multiple and contradictory truths that must be interrogated, particularly as they make manifest collective affective states, often resulting in our docility as political subjects. Pushing further, it is the *telling* of such truths—not simply the produced truths themselves—that warrant our critical analyses. Who gets to speak such truths, to make them visible? What does one need to do to be in a position to truth-tell? What is risked, or made more secure, in the telling?

As such, our political project might be one of risky truth-telling, a practice that operates differently from globalized neoliberal rationalities of extraction would offer. Given the ongoing development of schizo-society and the cultural paralysis that is its result, we need to engage in a different type of truth-telling, one that does more than reinscribe our schizophrenic state; we need a critically materialist truth-telling that risks the very subjectivities through which we are known, the very grounding through which we manage the contradictions of our schizo-society.

As I make clear in this chapter, I advocate for *parrhesiastic* methodological practices as a means for critical truth-telling. This productive orientation shifts the terrain through which key terms such as *methodological work, risk,* and *responsibility* are known. Indeed, the *parrhesiastic* orientation toward truth decidedly counters the tired hesitancy that has come to predominate the liberal world of methodological work, one that hesitates to invoke the term "truth" or "truths" for fear of essentializing or underdetermining experience, inference, or some element of confected reality.[3] The odd consequence of such hesitancy is that the inevitable tentativeness that extends from this nontruth positioning actually *enables* or furthers the proliferation of (contradictory) truths that are a hallmark of the schizo-society. We moved away from overt truth-telling to such a degree that we have achieved a type of methodologically induced paralysis—we've no truths upon which to act (or a landscape of multiple, overdetermined truths, the multiplicity of which makes it impossible for us to act). In this way methodologically informed relativism has a hand in the normalization of collective docility. We cannot remove ourselves from a shared responsibility for such consequences. We need to think, act, and live differently, according to new conceptions of responsibility and risk.

Methodological Consequences

Recall my earlier claims regarding methodological practice, risk, and responsibility as they extend from traditional and newly materialist positions. Operating as they do on a *logic of extraction,* traditional forms of qualitative research privilege a series of methodological techniques and procedures all aimed at removing subjects and phenomena from material contexts. Through this extraction, subjects and phenomena are "known," made visible as Certeau's (2011) *transportable objects,* or what is commonly referred to in methodological circles as data. Responsibility and risk draw meaning from the extractive imperative: it is one's responsibility to give *full* definition to the object of study, to relieve meaning of the residue of material context. In short, this means truncating the relational possibilities of such data *within* context by privileging understanding through extracted differentiation—meaning from *without*. Further, such extractive practices produce externalized truths—truth made visible through an analysis of external data, outside relation. As a consequence, this externalized truth is claimed as legitimate only if: (1) it sustains in some fixed fashion across time and space (as the post/positivists would have it), and (2) it is only tentatively linked to an immediate moment that cannot be understood in any broader sense (as the simplistic presentations of postmodern and/or standpoint theory might claim). There are obvious difficulties of both scenarios, with subsequent consequences for inquiry approaches in the name of political change and social justice. The first scenario results in truth as requiring a nearly faith-based belief in its stasis and foundational positioning beyond all contexts (yet nearly accessible from all contexts). Historically this approach has failed to hold up under the interrogations of poststructural theory: genealogical analyses show the production of such truths as sociohistorical in order and far from timeless or complete. The second scenario results in an unfortunate tendency toward relativistic thinking with encultured truths given equal standing regardless of moral outcomes. This approach fails the social justice project, as it lacks adequate grounding for progressive action. Keeping these inevitable shortcomings in mind, one might also inquire into the types of risks associated with each scenario.

Through the extractive production of meaning, the researcher only really runs the risk of intelligibility, of not making extracted data known to contemporary neoliberal norms and values. In this sense the extraction and analysis of data as fixed and complete asks the inquirer to link the same meaning to multiple contexts. Failure to do so would result in the disintegration of the extracted data as meaningful; analyzed data loses its productive hold when it fails the test of context. In the case of hyper-contextualized meaning, the researcher necessarily situates interpretive claims entirely within closed-off or otherwise partitioned contexts and hesitates to assert claims that extend beyond the momentary snapshot of the extracted setting. In both cases, of course, the researcher hardly engages in risky work. It is instead *normative* work—reproducing assumptions regarding timeless and relativistic meanings respectively. Risk in each case extends from concerns related to the production of data—one risks "losing data" or producing banal data that is "merely descriptive" of what we already know. These are not risks of anything on the ontological or epistemological level.

From an alternative view, the materialist focus outlined in Chapter 3 addresses the extractivist logic of traditional qualitative research through foregrounding relational knowing within an ongoing series of intra-actions. In this case methodological work encompasses the collapse of knowing into being, an onto-epistemological approach that posits that meaning is generated through the event of intra-active phenomena. The inquirer, then, remains entangled in a series of becomings—events that never conclude. These are decidedly material engagements that shift the inquiry project away from concerns regarding the proper extraction of knowable data to questions concerning the linkages and connections through which knowing and being are enacted. This focus on materiality reorients assertions of risk away from the data produced (data as product) toward a becoming data—one without definable end. Given the insights offered by the principles of new materialism, it remains important to consider how such a materialist approach might provide critical interventions into the normative production of extractive logics and practices: How, in short, might this materialist approach make available engagements in social justice work through inquiry? How might materially situated social justice work intervene within our globalized neoliberal context?

The neoliberal moment asks us to do more with less, to hold our individuality sacred and to make ourselves statistically normal in relation to a grand multiplicity (the double-bind of extractive logic, alluded to earlier, that informs credit scores). Principles of globalization assert the values of claiming an internal heritage that must be overcome in order to remain competitive within the global scale. This, it seems, is the postmodern *both/and* on steroids. We are meant to hold multiple contradictory truths in equal tension and do so without raising the alarm of abnormal function, of an inability to remain (economically) productive in the face of such circumstances. In short, we are meant to endure the schizo-society of multiple truths but remain unphased by the inevitable contradictions that develop from such contexts. Importantly, we have come to desire these contradictory formations—developing satisfaction from nearly reconciling them, from nearly (though certainly never fully) making them coexist without much visible friction.

The work of Deleuze and Guattari (1988) certainly points to this peculiar development as a distinct outgrowth of capitalism. Capitalism produces the schizo-society, as it needs—indeed, feeds on—schizophrenia for its continued expansion. Methodologically this plays out in somewhat interesting ways. Traditional inquiry approaches perhaps develop out of a similar contradictory relation—desiring the very subjects they simultaneously produce and consume, methodologies as outgrowths of desiring machines. This is an example of traditional research drawing from a neoliberal formation of capitalist values. Pushing this further, we can see the multiple ways in which truth and falsity are made to share the same stage (à la Buchanan's [2014] interpretation of the schizo-society)—methodological technologies (of research protocols or the sorting mechanisms of coding techniques) make visible findings that are rendered as "truths" because they come from legitimated methodological technologies. If truths are questioned, it is because they stem from outdated, inefficient, or misconstructed technologies. The impact of such truths—the ways in which they reify or call to question normative ways of being, for example—are rarely questioned.

Historically we might find the example of methodological traditionalists seeking to simultaneously show interpretive methods as both scientifically rigorous and not needing particularly scientific definitions of rigor for definition.[4] Consider also traditional coding mechanisms that encourage researchers to distill some narrated experience—to purify through breaking down—even as they intend to speak beyond the immediate codes. Often such codes are thematic representations—or metaphors—that stand in for the experience itself. They are not *the* experience; they point beyond themselves to *an* experience. Yet despite the very ambiguity that is metaphor—despite that metaphors, as metaphors, always extend beyond themselves—they are said to be somehow *more* precise, more definite, and thereby more meaningful than the experience they are meant to represent. It is as though the coding procedure was constructed to *nail down* meaning by *opening up* metaphor. This curious—some might say contradictory—scenario is activated by the need to order a sequence of events into meaning more than their surface.

Yet it is perhaps the absurdity of these multiple truth-falsities that draws one back to the comfort of standardized procedure. Through methodology we are able to make sense in ways that make sense. And, of course, we can do so without addressing the absurdity of our contemporary existence—without questioning our schizophrenic selves. Through the linear production of narration-coding-(re)presentation (to continue the example), we are given the comfort of ordered meaning, of logic where there otherwise might be non-sense. As a means to more productively engage—and more critically intervene—in the overproduction of truths, we perhaps need to think differently.

Renewed Critique

Though certainly offering his analysis in different terms, Foucault's (1997) reconceptualization of *experience* and *critique* stems from an engaged interrogation of neoliberalism as a rational system through which such limited notions of experience are known, even embraced, a concern I first raised at the beginning of this book. In response, Foucault considers experience as the ongoing interplay among truth, power, and relations to the self (Lemke 2011). Critique, Foucault offers, is engaging in problematization, insubordination, and the exposure of oneself as a subject. The intersection of these new assertions of critique and experience are important to understand as a background to Foucault's work on *parrhesia* as well as my own consideration of methodological responsibility and risk. Further, Foucauldian notions of critique decidedly counter the conflation of the term with simplified notions of criticism (as noted in Chapter 1).

An initial way to understand Foucault's notion of critique is his pivotal shift away from conceptions of the term as inherently negative, a perspective that entails deficit thinking and that distances the inquirer from the phenomena under study. In this way negative conceptions of critique emphasize procedures for locating and resolving errors of thought—contradictions and logical gaps in need of correction. This is the move toward synthesis inherent in dialectical inquiry. Further, in order to locate such deficiencies, there remains a necessary distance between the knower (one who produces the critique), the known (the object of critique), and the nonknower (those to whom the knower seeks to articulate a critique in the aim of edification). *Negative critique* thus begins from a place of differentiation.

In contrast to such negative formations, Foucault (1997) offers the productive possibilities of critique as a set of practices that locate the limits of truth regimes in order to extend beyond them (Lemke 2011). In this way critique refuses the limits of knowing and, instead, points to the possibilities inherent in indeterminate formations of being—of the yet-to-be-known. One engages in sustained critique of the historical present in order to allow new possibilities to open in the future. This is critique as employed by the criticalist of Chapter 1.

Similarly, Foucault's renewed notion of experience is one of extending beyond the limits of knowing, beyond the immediate present, and to a relational series of practices. In this sense experience is never "one's own" but manifests through the interplay of social practices with regimes of truth. One can never claim experience for oneself or as a marker for one's individual identity. Unlike the traditional conceptions of experience that inevitably fell short for Desjarlais (1997) as he sought to describe participant realities absent conceptualizations of a coherent internal subject, Foucault's notion of experience manifests through a series of relations—practices to practices, truth claims to truth claims—that are forever in the moment: experience as a practice of becoming.

Bringing this renewed notion of critique to bear on the relational conceptualization of experience means that the inquirer—s/he who engages in critique—is forever bound up within the *experiences that bear the weight of critique*. Critique is thus a relational act. Critique happens within, never without. As Lemke (2011) so succinctly asserts, "Critique means altering the 'rules of the game' while playing the game" (35–36). It is through the determined alteration of "the rules of the game" that the inquirer risks him/herself. Altering such rules necessarily alters the relations within the game—the interactions in which one is known, made visible, and understood. There thus exists the possibility—indeed, the hope—that critique will no longer allow the inquirer to be as s/he has been; critique impacts at the ontological level. Through critique one is able to identify the limits of ontological knowing—the limits of who one is—with the specific intention to transgress these limits, at risk to oneself. Thus, critique is risky stuff, exposing oneself to indefinite possibility. And, of course, because risk brings with it a degree of (productive) anxiety, critique is never simply an epistemological venture—critique takes place on the affective level of being. The political work of altering daily practices is dangerously powerful—dangerous because such shifts in practices are never predictable (Ross 2008) and powerful because they remain lodged in the materiality of the everyday. As depicted in Chapter 3, the relational approach of new or critical materialisms seeks to alter standardized "rules of the game" from the inside—refusing the distanced perspective of the spectator. As a consequence, such a critically informed materialism makes possible new practices for truth-telling, new ways for engaging in productive critique in the name of social justice.

Inquiry for social justice from the *parrhesiastic* perspective emphasizes re-lational means of knowing, coming to know, and being. An important part of this extends from elements of relational risk—inquirers need to risk the very relations that define them and give visibility/legitimation to their actions. In this sense inquiry-as-*parrhesia* requires a critical self-reflexivity of the inquirer, as s/he must continually develop truths in relation to multiple and overlapping contexts. Further, the *parrhesiast* can never fall back to the tentativeness of know-ing to refuse assertive truth claims—this is refusing the risk of truth-telling. The *parrhesiast* operates from an ethical duty to tell critical truths.

As Steele (2010) notes, in order to enact truth-telling from the position of the parrhesiast, "one needs the courage to oppose a community of which the *parrhesiates* ... is a member" (49). This remains of vital importance within the methodological community, as it combines methodological *critique* (interro-gating the normative means of coming to know—opposing the norms of the methodological community), *innovation* (making possible new forms of inquiry previously unavailable to normative onto-epistemological assumptions), and a sense of *ethical practice* (motivating one's opposition as a sense for achieving a more socially just society).[5]

Within Ancient Greece, status and practice played as much a role in the production of truth as did any cultural belief in an external or verifiable reality.

As Ross (2008) notes, "it is the *status* of the one who speaks, regardless of the dangerous implications of what they say, that determines whether they are speaking the truth" (62, original emphasis). Foucault linked this ability to tell the truth at risk to one's status to what we now know as the critical tradition in Western philosophy. However, it remains a specific element of critique that Foucault aligns with truth-telling—those who criticize the very practices they themselves enact. There is thus an element of acting/critiquing from within—no longer from the distanced without—in order to tell truths. These are the players of the game who actively seek to change the rules even as they play the game.

Because the *parrhesiast* allows truths to work on him/herself—to be affected by the very truths told and believed—s/he does not need to convince others of such truths (e.g., in the image of the rhetorician who must convince an audience of a truth even if s/he does not believe it) but instead is a moral exemplar that others may follow (Ross 2008). In this sense the intersection of belief in, knowledge of, and telling truth acts upon the *parrhesiast*: one is forever (and always again) altered by the engaged act of truth-telling that is *parrhesia*. Further, the *parrhesiast* does not necessarily see a truth that others do not but, instead, has the courage to speak truths that others choose not to see (Ross 2008). In this sense *parrhesia* extends from a radical *critique of the now* as well as a determination to make visible ways of being and knowing that otherwise escape critical notice. Simpson (2012) notes the simultaneous processes of recognition, conformation, and disruption inherent in *parrhesia*: politically subversive truth-telling must recognize immediate reality, conform with reality, and articulate alternative interpretations of that reality. This is the player who recognizes the rules of the game, alters his/her practices to meet the contours of such rules, and, at the same time, asserts changes to the rules as a means to make alternative, more socially just realities possible. Further still, the *parrhesiast* believes this process as "truth." Given Foucault's important reconceptualization of critique and experience, we might ask what this all means for how we understand methodological responsibility and risk.

In considering this early excavation of *parrhesia*, critique, and methodological work, I certainly recognize that no one text or author—critical though they might be—maps directly onto the practices and perspectives outlined in this chapter thus far. However, I do want to consider the productive role of three critical methodologists—Patti Lather, Ian Stronach, and Norm Denzin—who employ "radical critiques of the (methodological) now" in order to make new practices of an unknown future possible, important elements for *parrhesiastic* practice. By giving an overview of distinct selections of their work, I hope these authors serve as touchstones for methodological truth-telling and provide a jumping-off point for the more detailed examination of materialist methodologies as *parrhesia* that follows.

In *Getting Lost*, Lather (2007) employs a productive sense of critique, pushing against the limits of methodological truth regimes even as she exposes herself as a subject.[6] Through the work of her text Lather offers a "new geography where we are all lost to one degree or another" (161). Through unmooring scientific work from the grounding of traditional foundation, Lather posits an approach situated within "imperfect information where incompleteness and indeterminacy are assets" (161). Here foundational absence enables a differently engaged ethics, one that attends to the challenges of postmodernity even as it intervenes within the political now. This is truth-telling with no small amount of risk.

Specifically Lather's critique extends from an interrogation of clear speech and the network of power relations that enforce "clarity" as both rational and desired. In response, Lather offers truth as unspeakable, as in excess of those practices aimed at invoking clarity. As such, Lather notes the "violence of clarity," its "non-innocence" (86), and asks that we assume an engaged thinker/reader—an active relation within which we might speak—who productively encounters unspeakable truth. What, then, are the productive consequences of "getting lost," of critique that asks us to locate truth as in excess of the rational now? In practical terms Lather risked her relation to her participants, many of whom she notes as rejecting her attempts to render their realities in anything other than a linear progressive narrative. Thus, invitations to "get lost" are not always accommodated or even recognized—and just might be returned as a rejoinder to the original speaker. At the same time, Lather's attempts to practice a "double(d) science" offer distinct challenges to the methodological status quo.

Similar to Lather's presumption of an engaged thinker/reader, Ian Stronach (2010) seeks a reader "compelled to make rather than take meaning" (12). This is thus a relational means of knowing, a creative capacity that links reader-author-text-immediate now-and-possible future. As such, Stronach seeks to intervene in the logics that inform "a methodology determined in advance—the absolute convention of our times" (154). Such prescriptive approaches remain self-defeating, never risking political engagement beyond the most superficial of levels. As such, Stronach establishes his work as a necessary counter to contemporary methodological work, drawing as it does from traditional logics of containment: "methodology seeks to contain indeterminacies whereas we prefer to explore and mobilize them as far as possible" (146). Similar to Lather's work, Stronach points to the disruptive potential of excessive truths, those not governed by logics of extraction and, importantly, full of potential for political-material change.

Also like Lather, Stronach's insistent refusal to work from a place of the known—choosing instead to operate from the periphery of where already-known meets not-yet-known—risks his relation, in this case to his academic field. Thus it is that Stronach (2010) recounts how his presentation of a "becoming professional" as one who exploits the "tensions between 'economies of performance' and 'ecologies of practice'" had a disquieting impact on his field: "they did not go down well," even causing some members to term him a field-based "heretic" (121). For Stronach, this risky practice stems from a political call for inquiry to resist the kind of "educational death" that is implicit in contemporary trends toward the standardization and homogenization of curricula and pedagogical practice. Inquiry need not be swept up in the momentum of normalization; we need a different sense of truth-telling to counter and intervene within such trends.

Throughout his text Stronach (2010) engages in a written format that attends to a "performative ideal" (1). As a consequence, *Globalizing Education* is structured as a series of entangled "duets" rather than bound by a singular, progressive narrative of unification (121). This written practice perhaps attends to what Denzin (2010) terms the "new writing" that refuses to retell experience: "the telling creates the experience" (89). For Denzin, truth-telling extends to how we render both what we know and the event of knowing. There lies performative truth in such practices: "the goal is to change the world through the way we write about it" (90). Here Denzin follows in the tradition of Mills and Marx, to politically engaged scholars who famously sought critical projects to "change, not simply interpret, society" (9).

For Denzin, inquiry for social change begins from a politically ensconced performative project—truth-telling as deeply collaborative, dialogic practice. As such, Denzin (2010) begins from an openly political call for change: "I'll lay my cards on the table" (18). Through a vision of performative transformation, Denzin collapses forms of inquiry, activism, critique, and critical citizenship into a dynamic and shared process of truth-telling. Denzin's vision is utopic—granting space for considerations for being other than we currently are—and collaborative—inviting dialogic frameworks for multiple levels of social change, both local and global, individual and collective. Thus it is that Denzin calls for collective action toward social justice, the possibilities for radical democracy to insinuate a renewed vision of an emergent, socially just present. As noted a bit later in this chapter, *parrhesia* aligns with a *democracy of the immediate now* that assumes the possibilities inherent in a yet-to-be-determined future. Here Denzin's performative truths take on the political possibilities for radical change, a collaborative insistence on new ways for being and becoming. When read in relation, the works of Lather, Stronach, and Denzin point toward a *parrhesiatic* possibility—risky truth-telling with the aim of a more socially just, indeterminate future.

Parrhesia as Approach and Orientation

For a number of reasons, Foucault's interpretation of parrhesia interests me in terms of its subsequent implications for my own work as a scholar of methodology and methodological practices. Further, as Peters (2004) notes, Foucault's Berkley lectures late in life focused extensively on *parrhesia* as it relates to education, an area of study that I value for its potential to evoke social change even as I stand in awe of educational institutions' ability to reproduce social inequity.[7]

It is also worth recognizing that Foucault notes, almost as an aside in his lectures, the incompatibility of *parrhesia* with traditionally Cartesian epistemological claims that assume evidence as a type of mental fact (Foucault 2001). Given this, *parrhesia* could not occur in frameworks governed by a *logic of extraction*; instead, *parrhesia* must be situated within a worldview wherein truth-telling consists of embodied and materially situated activity. Thus, Foucault's interpretation of *parrhesia* is all the more important given the onto-epistemological orientation offered by the new materialism outlined in Chapter 3. The relational materiality asserted by new materialism makes possible new considerations for truth-telling, the possibility for *parrhesiastic* activity in contemporary times. Given the increasingly schizophrenic outcome of our cultural overproduction of truths, the critical approach of *parrhesia* is perhaps now all the more necessary for social change.

As such, I begin this section with a gloss of the principal elements of *parrhesia*. Next, I locate the necessary connections between *parrhesia* and a working democracy, pulling from my open stance that social justice work necessarily involves engaged democratic action. This linkage between truth-telling and democratic engagement corresponds with Foucault's differentiation between *political parrhesia* and *philosophical parrhesia*. Lastly, I end by pointing to how critical inquiry in the name of social justice might extend from the relational process of truth-telling exemplified by philosophical *parrhesiastic* work.

For Foucault, *parrhesia* is inherently political and begins from the position of productive social critique, making visible invested truths that disrupt normative ways of knowing and being in the world. As Foucault (2011) writes, the *parrhesiastic* standpoint "tries precisely, stubbornly, and always starting over again, to bring the question of truth back to the question of its political conditions and the ethical differentiation which gives access to it" (68). The emphasis on "political conditions and ethical differentiation" establishes a firm grounding within the immediate context even as it links truth-telling to the ever-shifting cultural terrain of political and ethical discourse. Contemporarily, critical methodologists can learn from Foucault's insistence on situating truth-telling and inquiry within a type of becoming social context, one that "always starts over again" from a newly emergent immediate context. In some ways this approach aligns with an insistence on processual analysis found in the work of Rosaldo (1993) and Resnick and Wolff (1987), among others—a shift from methodological engagements with objects or things to more critical interrogations of social processes that continually re-invent themselves. This "remaking of social analysis" (which is, of course, Rosaldo's subtitle) brings with it an important shift from methodological practices aimed at demystifying hegemonic culture to dismantling it, a shift more in line with the Foucauldian notion of critique offered earlier. Recall the inadequacy of social critiques that merely point out falsities within our cultural overproduction of truth; such critiques have failed the project of radical social change within our contemporary moment.

Simply put, to "tell the truth" is to begin anew, to remain deeply within the simultaneity of immediate material relations and historically discursive interactions that make the act of truth-telling possible. Far from a *logic of extraction, parrhesia* remains within the entanglement of related being and knowing—an onto-epistemologically grounded manner of living and knowing within the world. Importantly, Foucault (2011) seeks to differentiate his notion of truth-telling from technique: "*Parrhesia* is not a skill. . . . It is a stance, a way of being" (14). Herein lies a context where we methodologists might recognize the differentiation of method and methodology, of technocratic skills or techniques and considerations of approaches to knowing or coming to know. In this sense the methodological middle manager—s/he who simply operates the machinery of procedure—is not capable of this type of truth-telling. Indeed, Foucault's recognition of *parrhesia* as a "way of being" emphasizes the ontological orientation of truth-telling. More than isolating and presenting inquiry as an endless search for more tools in our methodological tool box, we need to practice and teach new ways of being in the world, new ontological orientations to meaning-making.

Thus, I advocate for the *parrhesiastic* stance as essential to qualitative inquiry in our contemporary moment, yet one that is often overlooked in deference to a normative fixation on technique and the separation of inquiry, method, data, and analysis from material contexts—a procedural sense of methodology that finds logical traction in the residue of extractive assumptions of knowing and being. As such, a commitment to *parrhesia* in qualitative inquiry changes how we teach and engage in critical qualitative inquiry. An overemphasis on technique in our graduate-level methodology courses necessitates a simultaneous—and counter-productive—distinction of prescribed methodological "steps" to the inquiry process. The inquiry process is thus extracted from the material realities of coming to know, and qualitative research is rendered apolitical. As "the methodologist" becomes a technician, expertise loses its political edge. To paraphrase Foucault (2011), the methodological technician can teach, but his/her teachings pose no risk; they merely ensure that technological knowledge survives, ready to be replicated by the student (soon to be technocrat). The classrooms we inhabit need to be more than the recreation of assembly lines of standardized method; instead, they need to take on the urgency of materially engaged workshops or laboratories, promoting yet-to-be-realized and deeply political elements of being, doing, and living.

Thus, I ask critical qualitative inquirers to consider their pedagogical and research projects as a materially situated and politically engaged processes of productive critique. As Foucault (2011) notes, "Revolutionary discourse plays the role of *parrhesiastic* discourse when it takes the form of a critique of existing society" (30). Truth-telling is born of critical engagement; inquiry as productive critique. For the *parrhesiast,* there can be no false distancing measures that separate the inquirer from the known or even processes of coming to critically know and be. More simply, enacting *parrhesia* means there can be no extraction of self, other, knowing, known, or being.[8]

Further, if we are to take Foucault's explication of *parrhesia* seriously, we must reconsider key concepts such as *methodological risk-taking* and *methodological responsibility,* considerations I return to later in this chapter. Indeed, from a *parrhesiastic* standpoint, dwelling within traditional formations of extractive logic is methodologically irresponsible, reifying the very approaches to knowing and coming to know that we perhaps seek to change.

Lastly, of course, I believe we need to refuse to shy away from that burdensome and often-heavy term of "truth." The *parrhesiast* dwells in truth-telling with the recognition that such actions are never fully figured, never contained or containable, and always in intrarelation to those material contexts that enable their production. Truths—and their telling—always begin again and within the phenomena they make visible. As responsible methodologists, then, we engage in theoretical questioning to make available previously unknown intra-actions of knowing and being. We engage in critically aligned methodological work to simultaneously trouble normative ways of meaning-making and provide the space for materially situated tactical formations of knowing, doing, and being.

Performing Truth

In order to best understand Foucault's definition of truth in relation to *parrhesia,* it is perhaps important to disentangle the relational qualities of such terms. To begin, "truth" is not to be understood as somehow the corollary of "real" nor the antithesis of "unreal." For Foucault, there is no real lived world that exists external to some humanist subject. Instead, it is perhaps more useful to understand *parrhesiastic* truth-telling in complementary relation to that of "fiction," as seen in the work of Simpson (2012). In this sense both truth and fiction act upon the present (*parrhesia* reveals a truth not currently recognized, and fiction presents an alternative view of the now), thereby altering the possible future; both truth and fiction make available possibilities that would otherwise remain foreclosed. Given my interest in materialist methodologies, this correspondence of truth and fiction offers unique possibilities when working with others who might seek to narrate some experience. Here the experience itself might be "true" if the telling acts upon the speaker and the listener. Further still, because the telling of the (true) experience can never be the experience itself, it is necessarily fictive: the telling is generated through a host of interpretations and rendering of experiences, always already removed from the experience itself. Whereas traditional methodologies perhaps sought to grow nearer to the actual experience unto itself, the materialist approach invoked by *parrhesia* shifts to understand how the telling affects normative knowing and being. In this way the methodologist can engage in *parrhesiastic* activity through speaking truths that are not already known, not already recognized by the present reality, even if they somehow seem fictive. This methodological engagement might assert something akin to what Simpson (2012) grants fiction: "a *proleptic* function, calling forth and enacting a new reality through its pronouncement" (105; original emphasis).

Further still, in place of creating predetermined definitions of truth, there remains an emphasis on the practice of truth-telling, immersing such an activity within distinctly materialist contexts: "Parrhesia works from a pragmatic truth—related to the temporal and spatial (community-based) context within which the parrhesiates speaks" (Steele 2010, 50). In order to achieve this element of truth-telling, one must interrogate the very temporal and spatial contexts that make this pragmatic truth possible. As a consequence, *parrhesiastic* practice necessarily begins with a critical examination of contemporary context—the very time and space that makes truth-telling possible. More than simply articulating some objective or timeless truth, practices of truth-telling from the *parrhesiastic* perspective pragmatically link truth to the material contexts that make the utterance possible—truth-telling as materially situated critique.

In many ways Foucault's account of *parrhesia* synchs with Denzin's (2003) relational conceptualization of *performance* and *performative*. As Simpson (2012) recognizes, *parrhesia* is more than simply being honest but is rather an act—or, more precisely, an enactment—of truth-telling. In this sense, *parrhesia* is performative in that it dwells in relationality, is never complete, and acts upon the contexts in which it becomes. No relation is ever unmoved by *parrhesia*: the telling-of-truth affects the teller, the listener, the relation that binds them, as well as the ontological possibilities of being through which we manifest in the world.

As Denzin (2003) writes, "*Performance* is an act of intervention, a method of resistance, a form of criticism. . . . Performance becomes public pedagogy when it uses the aesthetic, the *performative*, to foreground the intersection of politics, institutional sites, and embodied experience" (9; emphasis mine). Because of their relational enactment, performance and *parrhesia* never occur in isolation and never remain fixed in meaning. Further, Denzin's notion of performance invokes a refusal to reproduce normalizing truths. Instead, like the truth-telling of the *parrhesiast*, performance intervenes through refusing to reproduce what is already known, already seen. Importantly, as Denzin points out, we learn from performance as a type of "public pedagogy," and this learning is fully embodied even as it is fully political. In similar fashion, *parrhesia* exists as an enacted, embodied, and public truth-telling that begins through an act of public resistance. Refusing the already-told, normalized truths that reinscribe traditional ways of being, *parrhesia* as performance makes possible new ways of knowing, previously unseen modes of being and becoming within the world.[9] The overlap of Denzin's performance and *parrhesia* is key to the project for political change and social justice: *parrhesia* exists as the telling of truths that act upon truth itself—being itself, the teller and listener themselves. It is a performed truth that simultaneously changes the performed, the performer, and possibilities for future performances. In this vein the reason *parrhesia* is noted as "truth-telling" and not "truths-telling" or the like is that it is an in-the-moment performance that affects the now; it is an event that makes possible newly emergent enactments of truth-telling. Consequently, *parrhesia* can never be divorced from the enactment of truth-telling, the hyphen forever binding "truth" to "telling." It is simply too easy to try to isolate what was told as truth, to try to nail down what truth *is*. Instead, we need to think of truth along the lines of processual enactment—it is the telling that registers impact and makes possible what otherwise might remain foreclosed: truth-telling as a politically subversive and ethically situated event.[10] In his lectures on *parrhesia*, Foucault (2011) differentiates between performed "utterances" that produce assumed (and ordered) effects and *parrhesia* that proffers unknown, open, and thereby risky effects. In this way *parrhesia* interferes with the production of the present, disrupting traditional ontological and epistemological assumptions in order to allow all involved in relational truth-telling—tellers and listeners alike—to operate according to different circumstances of the now. Through this productive disruption, *parrhesia* remains politically subversive (Simpson 2012). This political enactment of truth-telling thus takes on important characteristics of "critical work" (first outlined in Chapter 1): *parrhesia intervenes*, thus becoming a social justice practice.

Parrhesia, Democracy, and Rhetoric

And yet given all that I have written thus far as I advocate for a *parrhesiastic* orientation of methodological work for social change, there remains an inherent danger in *parrhesiastic* actions regarding the work of the *parrhesiast* within the democratic sphere. Part of this would seem to stem from the aims of the *parrhesiast*: What is the goal of "telling the truth," and how does that goal coincide with democratic action? Foucault noted the necessarily contradictory relationship between *parrhesia* and democracy: democracy needs truth-telling in order to survive, yet elements of *parrhesia* might easily destroy democracy. Unfortunately Foucault's representation of malformed *parrhesia*—acts of truth-telling that counter democratic action—seem all too recognizable in our contemporary context. The danger lies in the practice of "telling the truth" as slipping into simple rhetoric. In this sense one engages in truth-telling solely to persuade one's audience in one direction or another. Drawing from Ancient Greek philosophy, Foucault (2011) notes that rhetoric dangerously separates belief from truth: through rhetoric one can claim select truths—or encourage one's audience to particular conclusions regarding truth—without actually believing the truth itself. In this way the rhetorician is driven by the Greek notion of *techne*, or employing skills. This causes Foucault to emphasize two different approaches to *parrhesiastic* practice among the Ancient Greeks: (1) *political parrhesia*, which all too easily becomes the province of the rhetorician; and (2) *philosophical parrhesia*, which links truth with belief and, consequently, exists as an ethical stance in relation to the world. Importantly both practices have a pivotal role to play in democracy—one manifests through persuading the populace toward some end, and the other with calling to question the very realities that give sense to everyday democratic practices. However, whereas the former approach creates false democratic action, the latter makes space for radical democratic engagements. It is thus through *philosophical parrhesia* that we might locate critical inquiry practices for social justice.

Democracy requires an engaged populace, one that deliberates on discussions of what is true and what is false. As noted earlier, acts of *parrhesia* necessarily call to the fore immediate truths that, in turn, alter the very logics that inform daily practices. However, it remains important to note that an inability to distinguish truth from falsity (or giving equal standing to multiple, contradictory truths, as is the case with the schizo-society) necessarily imperils democracy. Stagnated democracy—devised of a populace paralyzed by the multiplicity of undifferentiated truths—loses its critical possibility: it cannot significantly change, repeating the same practices, beliefs, and values across time and space, regardless of context. These are the circumstances of a society that relies on extractive logics, Cartesian cuts in the formation of meaning. The critical interventions of *philosophical parrhesia*, however, orient toward truths that, through their telling, require change, shifts in the patterns of being and knowing. In this way *parrhesia* is doubly dangerous to democracy. In the conservative first sense, *political parrhesia* destroys democracy by enforcing social stagnation and repetition. Here there is no room for political projects for social change; there lies only incremental changes to what is already seen, what is already known. This is the province of the methodological technocrat and might be deemed a *democracy of the past*—reforming what already was. However, in the more liberatory second sense, democratic activity stems from an engagement with an immediate yet unfinished now. This is a becoming democracy that requires sustained, reflective critique with the aim of social change. This is the province of *parrhesiastic* activity. The *democracy of the immediate now* risks truths that *require* change. As a result, the *democracy of the immediate now* is disrupted toward a yet-to-be-realized future. This version of *parrhesia* necessitates an ethical commitment toward social justice through radical democratic action. *Parrhesiastic* methodologies contribute to such democratic action through linking daily practices to the logics that inform them, with the hope that such critical action makes previously unknown truths visible—and, in their visibility, they change. The relational materiality of *parrhesia* is thus an openly engaged intervention, a practice of radical democratic action.

In relation to the terms emphasized throughout this book, *political parrhesia* might be understood in line with the extractivist logic considered in Chapter 2. In particular, there would seem to be a correspondence between Frankfurt's (2009) notion of the "bullshitter" and Foucault's rendition of the rhetorician in ancient times. Recall that one who engages in "bullshit" does so without regard for truth—the bullshitter disregards truth in favor of persuasion. (Recall also that Frankfurt deemed the bullshitter more dangerous than the liar, as this latter person at least recognizes a truth before speaking an avowed nontruth; the bullshitter simply does not care about the truth.) In similar fashion, the danger of the rhetorician within the political sphere is that s/he disregards any sort of truth—an epistemological stance of disinterest toward knowing—and seeks only to persuade. As such, *political parrhesia* quickly works against democracy or any sense of progressive/radical democratic change, as the goals of truth-telling are severed from belief: it doesn't matter what you believe, it doesn't matter if you believe what you say; what matters is that you persuade your audience. At times our current news cycle might give one pause to consider whether our politicians simply employ a form of *political parrhesia*—aiming to persuade their constituents of some "truth" to which they are persuadable.[11] This is truth-telling as pure skill: there is no question of belief (it does not matter if I believe it or not; I simply aim to persuade you), only the rhetorical techniques of truth-telling (or, of course, the rhetorical skills of bullshit).

Recall for a moment my claims in Chapter 2 that much of the methodological work these days disappointingly emphasizes techniques—mechanisms for persuading one's audience that one's assertions are valid or true—at the expense of utilizing the position of truth-telling to promote some element of progressive change in the name of social justice. In crass terms, I suppose, we methodologists have become skilled at bullshit. In more philosophical terms, I would argue that traditionalist methodological orientations emphasize a *political parrhesia* that all too easily slips into an overemphasis on *techne* even as it divorces belief from truth-telling. This slippage often occurs pedagogically as well. The "methods course" overemphasizes *techne* as the instructor seeks to persuade students to utilize some normative "best practice," feeding a learned student the desire to "do research" correctly.

In counter-distinction, Foucault's claims regarding *philosophical parrhesia* emphasize an ontological view in which, in his terms, truth and belief "coincide." Here the emphasis remains on telling-the-truth not with a goal of "what to do" (which is the province of the persuasive rhetorician) but rather "who to be" (which is the province of the philosopher). Further, *philosophical parrhesia* extends the intersection of government and the care of the self. Whereas the *parrhesiastic philosopher* used to focus on the care of the prince's soul, s/he now emphasizes practicing philosophy—insinuating a care of the self even as s/he tells others how to care for themselves. There is a harmony here between speaking and living, an authentic relation to one's own self that continues through to the words one speaks. This is *parrhesia* as a philosophico-ethical stance toward the world, an ethically engaged means of truth-telling. Further *philosophical parrhesia* points to a different type of disruption to normative political functioning within a democracy. Whereas *political parrhesia* perhaps leads to rhetorical interventions aimed at producing a social change that per-suades select groups to think alike (and, further, follow-alike, hence the advent of facism), *philosophical parrhesia* makes available a type of civic disobedience that derives from the very linkage of belief and truth-telling.

Reclaiming Truth-Telling in Methodological Practice: *Parrhesiastic* Work

So what, then, does this all have to do with methodology? Well, my concern with the *logic of extraction* stemmed from (1) the overemphasis on the development of methodological skill, procedure, and activity, all aimed at extracting "things" from contexts or events; (2) the ease with which this positions the methodolo-gist as, at best, a technocrat or middle manager and, at worst, a bullshitter; (3) the inability of extractivist logics to instigate any real political change—like *political parrhesia*, those extractivist logics that inform traditional methodolo-gies unduly separate belief from practice, the ethical from being or becoming. Moving toward a materialist perspective opens the possibility to resituate the inquirer within the phenomena of interest—inquiry is recognized as imbued within the event it seeks to understand. Yet mine continues to be a call for an activist approach to inquiry, one that intervenes in the name of social justice. Similarly, Steele's (2010) assertion of *parrhesia* within the academy as neces-sarily activist aligns with his claims that the object of truth-telling need not be motives or intentions but instead the logic formations or rationalities that inform our academic practices—the values and/or "practices of theorizing" that most directly inform our inquiry practices (60). Hence the importance of maintaining methodological work as, at the same time, philosophical work.

Because I am not ready to foreclose on the notion of truth-telling, I find it useful to consider methodological practice alongside Foucault's notion of *par-rhesia*. In this way I seek next to situate critical methodological approaches to inquiry as a type of *parrhesiastic* work. To be clear, I do not believe there is any way to fully match *parrhesia* as enacted during the time of the Ancient Greeks with contemporary manifestations of qualitative inquiry; a one-to-one corre-spondence is not my aim. Instead, I want to consider *parrhesia* as an approach to living, being, and knowing the world differently—more productively—than we have traditionally as well as the implications that such a shift might have for those of us who take seriously the goals and aims of critical methodological practice. Given the useful onto-epistemological shifts afforded by the perspec-tive of new materialism (discussed in Chapter 3), I find congruent threads that, together, imply a progressive orientation for what inquiry can be and what it, in turn, asks of the inquirer. If a *parrhesiastic* orientation toward the world is not possible given our overreliance on Cartesian epistemologies (as Foucault suggests), perhaps the new materialist reconfiguration of the world provides a helpful opening for considerations of inquiry that are more parallel with ancient associations of truth-telling than not. In short, this next section is my way for thinking through the intersections of inquiry, social justice work, and a relational onto-epistemological stance to the contemporary world.

To begin, Foucault's (2011) interpretation of *parrhesia* involves three relational elements: *citizenship, responsibility,* and *risk*. Importantly, each of these elements is foregrounded in particular ways and collude to make possible truth-telling as an orientation toward or means of being in/with the world. Further still, the particular manifestations of citizenship, risk, and responsibility derive from a relational understanding of the world, one that usefully corresponds with the relationality implied by new materialism. As a means for understanding the linkages among *parrhesia* and inquiry, I would like next to consider these three elements as asserted in Foucault's rendering of truth-telling.

First, the *parrhesiast* can only "tell the truth" if s/he is a recognizable member of a community: the *parrhesiast* speaks—and is heard—as an identifiable citizen. Though this had particular manifestations in Ancient Greece (we know, for example, that only select groups of people could actually participate in the democratic sphere; most notably, women and slaves were excluded from engaging in public discourse), I think it important to consider in relation to methodology. Though some might read this as a secondary point, I find it important that those of us studying, writing, and teaching about inquiry assert our position as methodological scholars. In doing so, we must necessarily position ourselves as methodologists in particular ways. As a consequence, we might usefully ask: How do we define ourselves as methodologists? What does it mean to engage in methodological work? How is it that others define us as members of a particular community, as active citizens in simultaneously local groupings and more macro-oriented fields? More than simply invoking the privilege of position, this is simultaneously claiming a space from which to speak, a productive capacity to locate and engage with a position of active citizenship. Further still, I would like to consider the specific position of the critical inquirer—one whose methodological work is aimed at intervening within, not solely describing what are, the normative rationalities that have such hold on our contemporary moment.

Indeed, at times it seems that our methodological neighbors—those who consider quantitative methodologies—are more easily situated as "methodologists." This is to say that methodological identity seems to follow claims concerning degrees of expertise—"I am a statistician"; "s/he is a psychometrician." Regard-less of one's position concerning professional identity, it remains important to acknowledge the multiple zones from which one speaks, to recognize our own privilege of citizenry as, say, faculty in educational institutions, members of par-ticular fields of study, and contributors to more localized communities and the like. The importance of this self-positioning stems from ethical claims that with the privilege of citizenship comes a responsibility to actively engage and speak out from/to the very communities that afford us our recognition. This active citizenship is an important element of *parrhesia*, as one's truth-tellings are made visible from the very groups through which we draw an identifiable positioning. Linking critical methodologies with a type of active citizenship perhaps makes possible the production of critical citizenship, a performed engagement that Roberts (2014) recognizes as created through a shared responsibility to critique and examine alternatives to the ontological and epistemological status quo.

Second, one comes to the practice of truth-telling from a responsibility to speak truths as one knows them. This is to say that the *parrhesiast* makes no at-tempt to occlude or otherwise hide the truths s/he understands or lives. Further, the truths one has a responsibility to speak are always oriented toward some power or governing structure. This element of power is strikingly important and linked to a Foucauldian (re)consideration of power from disciplinary to biopower. Whereas power, for Foucault, used to reside within some sovereign subject, contemporary formations of power are more dispersed, extending through principles of governmentality. So how, then, does this reconsideration of power affect or otherwise implicate *parrhesiastic* methodological practice? Instead of simply speaking a truth to the prince or king, the *parrhesiast* has a responsibility to truth-tell to the multitude of institutions, practices, and identities through which power manifests. As such, truth-telling can never be fully complete; as Foucault maintains, "we always have work to do." Herein lies an important distinction between *parrhesia* as it manifested in Ancient Greece as compared to our contemporary moment. As Foucault (2011) explicates, *parrhesiastic* work as it first developed was oriented toward a particular person or role. In this way the truth-teller addressed a particular (and identifiable) subject (most often the prince). As it now stands, however, there is no purely constituted subject—power manifests differently. As such, the *parrhesiast* is differently oriented—toward practices, institutions, and rationalities, not select people or things. This brings with it, of course, a different conception of the risks associated with truth-telling.

Third, because the *parrhesiast* engages in truth-telling from a particular posi-tion as a citizen, s/he risks the very relations through which s/he is known by telling the truth. As originally construed, the *parrhesiast* risked his/her own life when telling the truth—truths were critiques of the prince or king, as the one in power did not see or understand them on their own (if they did recognize such truths on their own, they would not need the *parrhesiast* to speak them). Thus the *parrhesiast* tells the truth all the while recognizing that such acts might cast him/her out of relation; the *parrhesiast* risks the very relations through which s/he is known. Given our contemporary context, differing conceptions of relation imply a different sense of risk. One risks one's citizenship, one's relation in particularly new ways. Importantly, *parrhesiastic* truth-telling is never independent of context; indeed, as Steele (2010) points out, such truth-telling activities extend from "counter-power," challenging the very regimes of truth that grant us our voice. Within the world of academe, *parrhesiastic* critics use the disciplinary language afforded them to critique the very discipline that grants them their status. As an extension, part of the momentum to engage in activist work is to disrupt the normalizing conventions that give the academic his/her privilege.

Putting this all together, then, shows the means by which the *parrhesiast*, through truth-telling, simultaneously stakes a claim (and is recognized as belonging) to citizenship all the while risking the very set of relations that make him/her visible (as a citizen) in the first place. In this way the *parrhesiast* seeks to transform the relations of which s/he is a part—the telling of truths makes possible an ongoing array of relational possibilities (some anticipated, perhaps, and some not) and, as a consequence, is an intervention into the reproduction of standardized meaning. The *parrhesiast* never fully knows—never could fully know—the outcome of truth-telling, and as such, each *parrhesiastic* activity carries with it some degree of (productive) risk.

Of course, these three elements of citizenship, responsibility, and risk find definition from traditional approaches to research as well—these are not solely the province of *parrhesia*. However, renewed onto-epistemological assumptions inform more useful and productive ways for understanding such terms and the practices they make possible. What the *logic of extraction* teaches us is the ease with which methodological citizenship translates to that of the middle manager or technocrat; that is, the methodologist becomes known, made visible through the means by which s/he manages the technological apparatus associated with research—this is citizenship by technical expertise. As the example shows, though the extractivist methodologist might find a place among the citizenry, s/he could never claim the role of active, critical citizenship. As such, traditional methodological approaches foreclose on the transformative possibilities inherent in critical truth-telling; a fixation on technique trumps considerations of methodological citizenship in the name of social change or justice.

Within the context of a globalized neoliberalism, the technocratic method-ologist draws worth through demonstrating technical proficiency, the ability to produce codified meaning more effectively and efficiency. This is making-meaning known by and to the normative systems that abound. In this sense the methodologist is responsible for reproducing meaning—for its extraction, analysis, and re-articulation according to normalized systems of logic. As such, methodological practice poses little to no risk to the methodologist him/herself and certainly little risk to the institutions that grant him/her definition and visibility. In short, considerations of citizenship, responsibility, and risk remain firmly oriented toward the technologies with which the methodologist works. Obviously this remains in stark contrast to Foucault's notion of the *parrhesiast,* who engages in truth-telling activities that, through their very activation, risk the methodologist him/herself.

Conclusion

Truth-telling is risky business. At the same time, educational research, stripped of material contexts and governed by principles of extracted technique, fails any political project for change. We are in a time of normative methodological practices that dwell in extraction and procedurization. Mine is a call for critical qualitative inquiry in education as *parrhesiastic* work. In practice, considering the methodological possibilities of *parrhesia* requires critical researchers to de-vote the energies of inquiry to those practices that could never be understood according to the *logic of extraction*—that is, those practices of living/being that remain unaccounted for by the governing logic of our times. This might be done by looking for the traces of immovable being within the transportable, what we all too easily deem "data." This is the imprint of the everyday that can never be fully scrubbed from interpretation. In my own work I strive to recognize such traces through an ongoing examination of embodiment and emplacement, mate-rial processes that might challenge easy claims of "data" and "analysis." Through this work I find that the risks of critical materialism are striking and real. Yet it is this commitment to risk, to truth-telling as political action via inquiry, that makes *parrhesia* so vital to qualitative methodology. Through taking the stance of the material *parrhesiast,* critical qualitative inquirers might more productively interrogate educational processes and practices absent the crutch of extraction. Alongside this, of course, is a renewed sense of being and knowing in the world.

The *parrhesiast* cannot abide by relations between, acting instead within the very truths s/he makes visible. As Barad (2007) so eloquently articulates, this matters "since the possibilities for what the world may become call out in the pause that precedes each breath before a moment comes into being and the world is remade again, because the becoming of the world is a deeply ethical matter" (185). Because of the ongoing, relational orientation of *parrhesia*, it can never be understood outside of a decidedly moral orientation toward impactful and intentional social change. This results in a heightened sense of both responsibility (to the self and others) and risk (of the self to others). As Simpson (2012) writes, "because one not only possesses *parrhesia*, but also enacts it regularly as part of the relationship one has to both truth and others, it bears with it both a high degree of responsibility and risk" (101). The *parrhesiast* speaks truths that are contrary to what is known, a reality that does not naturally extend from normative ways of knowing and being.

And so I would like to end this chapter by revisiting those questions that have been sprinkled throughout this book thus far—not to prescribe answers but instead to point to how the incorporation of the relational approaches of Certeau's *tactical knowledge formations* (seen in Chapter 2), Barad's *critical materialism* (Chapter 3), and Foucault's explication of *parrhesia* (this chapter) overlap to bring newly productive meaning to their formations. What risks must we take with our data and in our inquiry process to "tell the truth"? This is about reorienting ourselves within the inquiry process toward tactical formations of knowledge and relational ways of being. How do our assertions, our truth-telling, imperil or destabilize our very relation to our assumed other and the normalized identities we hold most dear? This is about methodological practices intimately entangled with practices of being and knowing (ontological and epistemological practices and assumptions) and the tentativeness of our citizenship within our confected world. How might such destabilization, such risk-taking, be productive in the sense that it makes available new ways of knowing or previously unavailable ways of coming to know? This is about reorienting to the unknown, how intrarelation (within) makes newly possible that which interrelation (without) could never attain. Lastly, how might a materialist methodological approach require particular risks of the inquirer that are lost in traditional extractivist approaches to qualitative inquiry? This is about refusing extraction and locating materialism as a politically charged way of knowing and coming to know.

Chapter 5

Methodological Materiality: Toward Productive Social Change

Introduction: Inquiry Beyond Technique

I no longer want to have debates about what I term the "tool-box approach" to inquiry. Phenomenological inquiry or grounded theory or ethnographic work is not about which wrench to use on what type of pipe or whether one should use a hammer or a screwdriver in particular methodological-improvement circumstances. These are examples of reducing methodology to the level of procedure, and my concern is that our conversations regarding methodological responsibility have become unnecessarily procedurized, as though discussions at the level of technique are a way forward to any sort of real change in education inquiry. At best, maintaining our discussion of inquiry at the level of technique is a bit intellectually lazy. (I am not a technocrat; my interest in methodology is not to play the role of some sort of research-based middle manager.) At worst, this limiting fixation on technique is dangerous. This chapter is about that danger as well as the promise of *parrhesia* as an activist approach to inquiry—truth-telling for political change.

Tool-box approaches emphasize maintaining or perhaps making more efficient those structured ways of coming to know that are already imagined to exist; they deal with codified knowledge systems. In this way they fail to promote

The Responsible Methodologist: Inquiry, Truth-Telling, and Social Justice, by Aaron M. Kuntz, 121–142.

research practices that might intervene in any real way beyond the level of *techne*. Further still, tool-box approaches reinforce traditionally patterned assumptions about knowing, coming to know, and being—they reinscribe normative ontological and epistemological claims. As such, the reduction of methodological discussions to questions of which tools to pull out of one's tool-box fails any attempt at conducting inquiry in the name of social justice. There is no vision for yet-to-be-established moments of change, no openness to a future that is not already known. In this way our overemphasis on procedure or technique within the methodological community continually falls short when considered within discussions of instigating progressive social change.

Herein lies the danger of such a simplistic approach: from an ontological and epistemological level, the tool-box approach can only repeat normative claims on being and knowing. And, in re-asserting such standardized visions of the world, the tool-box approach validates systems of inequality that critical scholarship seeks to change. In many ways Peim's (2009) assertions regarding the "crisis of method in educational research" make a similar point:

> It can be said that there is a crisis of method in educational research, but certainly not a shortage. Handbooks, guides, research training programmes abound. Major publishing houses commission manuals for educational researchers. There is rather a fear that all this proliferation, all of this charting and tabulation of method ends up promoting a dull, menu-bound research that suffers from lack of creativity and vision. (241)

The proliferation of methods texts perhaps points to the expansion of educational research as a technical field. As research methods become more technically precise—requiring an advancement in technical expertise for their employment and understanding—more, it seems, is better. And yet what is lost in this expansive advancement on the technical front? How might this excited extension of method crowd out other, more socially engaged concerns? Indeed, if inquiry is to play a role in activating progressive social change, it will occur through the very openness of creativity and vision that traditional tool-box approaches deny.

Given the ubiquity of textbook manuals, all dealing with what Peim terms the "charting and tabulation of method," it makes good sense to interrogate both how we came to this point and how we might tack a different course, one that begins with the need for inquiry practices themselves to provoke new relational ways of being, possibilities for living differently. It remains our responsibility as methodologists to provoke the intimate link among inquiry and living—questions of inquiry necessarily involve questions of being. Involving questions of ontology in research debates establishes inquiry firmly within the realm of the political. The assumptions we make regarding inquiry matter.

As such, methodologists can no longer absent themselves or their methodological work from larger philosophical and political debates on knowing and being. A challenging first step is a collective refusal of the myths of neutral or objective methodological practices, enacted by disinterested technicians. Importantly, this step away from neutrality as a necessary ideal (both in methodological and overt political practice) must *not* signal a simultaneous turn toward relativistic claims on reality—that my positionality only allows me to comment on my most immediate cultural context; rather, critical inquirers invested in social change must invoke a relationally engaged practice of truth-telling that is politically risky and ethically responsible. In short, relational means of knowing necessarily refute misinformed denouncements of relativism (after all, if we are always in relation, then your claims and practices always affect mine, if even from an entangled distance). Further still, principles of relationality refute claims of objective distance—I am always implicated by the analyses I enact and therefore can never be detached from the weight of their critique.

More than some promising practice for activist scholarship, locating and operating within a politically informed position is simply good research practice. As Kuhn (2008) writes, neutrality in research is a misplaced ideal:

> Underpinning any research activity are the basic assumptions of the researcher about the nature of 'reality' and the way we comprehend it. Ideas about knowledge, about what we can know (an ontological concern) and how we can know it (an epistemological question), long central to philosophical reflection, guide research. So too do beliefs, values (axiological concerns) and aspirations. (179)

Given this, methodological scholars would do well to emphasize interrogations of the very "ideas about knowledge" that emerge within select sociohistorical contexts and make possible particular methodological orientations and accepted research practices. Indeed, it is the role of the critical methodologist to take such assumptions and the practices they make possible as a field-based area of investigation; these comprise the content areas that separate the methodologist from the technocratic middle manager of normative methods. This situates research within historical contexts, produced from the very norms that give them common-sensical meaning. As Kuhn goes on to write, it is perhaps most useful "to regard research as activity undertaken by socially interacting individuals employing various frames of reference that orient meaningful activity. Research in this formulation is constituted by and embedded within discourses, thereby creating an identifiable culture of inquiry" (179). I might add to Kuhn's assertions that such activity, "constituted by and embedded within discourses," is *materially* situated, with very real material consequences.

Rudolph's (2014) interrogation of research practices in education usefully addresses the material intimacy of research approaches, assumptive educational contexts, and pedagogical practice. As Rudolph notes, an overreliance on the experimental model as a "gold standard" for educational research has rather alarming consequences for not only methodological practices but also the realm of policy, pedagogy, and curriculum as well. In the words of Rudolph:

> If we believe that progress can be made in education only if we embrace something similar to the experimental models of physics, medicine, or agriculture, then to get these models to work in the real world requires us to constrain our educational activities so that they more closely match the research models we use to generate knowledge. We would need to, in other words, make the naturally occurring system more like the experimental system, a change that would require the simplification of natural learning environments. This might entail things like the standardization of learning goals, scripted instructional plans, the reduction of individual and institutional autonomy, and so on. Only by extending the conditions of the laboratory to the setting we seek to improve can the power of knowledge produced in that context be realized. (17)

Unfortunately, many educators, administrators, students, and critical inquirers alike can testify to the multiple ways in which the experimental model maps onto and, indeed, alters the educational environment in rather confining ways. In an odd way methodological mandates that require classrooms more like "experimental systems" lead to and extend from an intensification of technocratic research procedure. As "natural learning environments" are simplified to meet experimental research assumptions, the methods themselves become more complex. Thus, there are consequences for our methodological practices that extend beyond the confected boundaries of our research studies. Indeed, methodological work brings with it a host of assumed logic formations. As Peim (2009) writes, "No educational research exists without some—explicit or implicit—reliance on ideas about the specific world of practice it addresses that in turn depend on ideas about the nature of the 'world' in the larger sense" (237). These assertions about what we know, how we come to such knowledge, and how we live affect both the findings we devise *and* the research encounter-event itself. This is the relational import of the time in which we find ourselves. As such, those research acts that draw from *logics of extraction* have a hand in, as Rudolph notes, making phenomena themselves "more like the experimental system," thus unnecessarily reducing to stasis otherwise dynamic relations. Of course, different from Rudolph, I would argue that the implied distinction between "natural" and "artificial" contexts is not as important as that between determinations of phenomena as imbued with a material relationality or extractive stasis, of taking a materialist methodological stance or assuming a *logic of extraction* respectively. As a consequence, we need to engage in methodologies built on political acts of truth-telling, methodological practice as *parrhesia*.

As Peim (2009) advocates, "questions of method are not simply questions of craft but are always also questions engaging metaphysics—in other words, they are questions concerning ideas about how things are" (236–37). At issue, I think, is the conflation of "questions of method" with "questions of craft" (those of technique, expertise, and product, to name but a few) at the expense or occlusion of Peim's definition of metaphysics. That is, we need to continue to recognize that attempts to shape the "craft of research" are simultaneously attempts to think and enact inquiry differently, with all the consequences and possibilities that extend from such power-laden actions.

This is difficult work: tool-box approaches to method are seductively simple, requiring as they do only a detailed understanding of what is already known and experienced; in this simplification lies its seduction. The tool-box approach foregoes the possibility of critique in favor of the certainty of method. Through the intensification of certain methods, methodological identity comes to the fore—the methodologist lays claim to the privilege of expertise. In this way a fixation on methodological work as simply producing better tools and refining techniques to employ those tools aligns disappointingly well with the governing rationalities of our contemporary moment—the very rationalities that I propose throughout this book as needing to be interrogated and changed in the name of social justice.

Given our contemporary moment of globalized neoliberalism, it remains all the more difficult to engage in critical investigations that extend beyond the reductive space of technique. As Davies (2010) notes, "Neoliberalism is founded on a strong assertion that *there is no alternative*, making critique redundant" (65, original emphasis).[1] As such, the very act of critique (in the Foucauldian sense of the term) is radical, indeed, challenging neoliberal norms as the definitive values of our present and future times. With this in mind, if we seek to invoke some element of change, we need to challenge our existing assumptions about how we come to know and how such knowing affects how we operate within the world in which we live. Davies notes this is a "struggle against oneself, against the normative force of language and everyday practice. It is a continuous struggle" (58).[2] In many ways, then, this book is an example of my own struggle against myself—I seek to challenge my own adherence to *logics of extraction* and do so with the belief that critical inquiry practices might enact more socially just possibilities for a future that is yet to be known, yet to be lived. Critique makes alternatives possible.

As such, throughout this book I have sought to present several critiques, the process of which makes newly possible select principles, practices, and orientations toward qualitative inquiry for social justice. These critiques began with an interrogation of the *logics of extraction* as outlined in Chapter 2. Extractivist logics bring with them a host of consequences for inquiry generally (assuming stable fixity of knowing and coming to know, linear progressions of experience, technocratic expertise as methodology, to name but a few) and social justice work more specifically (that change can be measured or instigated through advancements in technique, that social justice can occur in isolation at the level of the individual, that researchers may remain outside of the very contexts they seek to study, etc.). In response, I offered the relationally based assumptions of materialism and the contemporary assertions of being and knowing within phenomena found in new or critical materialism, outlined in Chapter 3. Principles of materialism refuse extractivist logics, recognizing instead a dynamic relationality that displaces Cartesian cuts for materially ensconced and fluid presentations of meaning-making. This shift toward relational materiality requires newly designed inquiry practices; methodologies once informed by extractivist logics no longer make sense. Further, the very goals of inquiry for social justice shift and change given the onto-epistemological assumptions of relational materiality.

On one level, relational materiality refuses any claim that radical change can occur in isolation, distanced or set off from the entangled relations through which phenomena manifest. In some ways this materialist emphasis on relational change aligns well with Willis's *Learning to Labor* (1977), wherein he notes the seduction of individual-level conceptions of change:

> To the *individual* working class person mobility in this society may mean something. Some working class individuals do 'make it' and any particular individual may hope to be one of them. To the class or group at its own proper level, however, mobility means nothing at all. The only true mobility at this level would be the destruction of the whole class society. (128, original emphasis)

Importantly, as Willis points out, the privileging of individualistic approaches to change has an impact on daily practices, particularly in education: "It is in the school with its basic teaching paradigm that those attitudes needed for *individual* success are presented as necessary in *general*" (129, original emphasis). In this way the school follows a logic of individualism that assumes corresponding values among administrators, teachers, and students alike. As such, individualist logics and values collude with assumed practices to promote select student identities as successful (those who conform) or deficient (those who deviate from such norms). This is the means by which institutionalized values and beliefs inform or otherwise make usefully visible everyday practices. In this way one might recognize a correspondence among select methodological values (institutionalized via the "dull, menu-based research" that Peim decried earlier) and particular practices of method. Individualized "promising practices" of research thus become "necessary in general." Of course, one might extend Willis's analysis by pointing more directly to the ease with which individualistic logics (asserted in more contemporary times by the hyper-capitalistic nature of neoliberalism) sever relational contexts; the individual is distinguished through extractive circumstance. In response, a materialist reading points to the inherent contradictions of such logical claims—individualistic and extractive logics fail when considered relationally, once common-sensical practices lose their logical traction. This allows Willis to reveal the ways in which educational systems privilege individual values (in this case, of mobility between socioeconomic categories) as necessarily informing the assumed values of the larger community, creating an array of "logical" daily practices. The result is an equally necessary contradiction: such values (i.e., of mobility) only make sense at the individual level. Increasing the scale of the process to that of the community or class relations shows that collective/relational mobility is not possible in the present system. Hence the need for the educational apparatus to encourage—one might say indoctrinate—perceptions that remain fixed at the individual level.

And, of course, it is perhaps easy to translate this contradiction of scale to methodological work. The theoretical orientation of poststructuralism, for example, grants an interpretive logic of moving from one scale (say, that of individual meaning-making) to another (say, of the discursive formations of institutions) to recognize how the latter informs the former—and the ways in which the former (practices), in turn, give credence or visibility to the latter (institutions). This leads Foucault (1991) to famously claim that his "target of analysis" was *practices*, "with the aim of grasping the conditions which make these acceptable at a given moment" (75). "Conditions," of course, extend beyond the immediacy of the actual practice. From the traditional methodological perspective (drawing as it does from globalized neoliberal values), such conditions are excessive—they need not be addressed in research practice. The individual scale, severed from other relations, informs a limited orientation.

As a consequence, cutting one scale from another (often in the guise of technical specificity) is shown from the materialist orientation as methodologically limiting and phenomenally simplistic.

Further still, a critical or new materialist orientation to inquiry might seek to understand the very contradictions noted by Willis in the production of individual and class-based mobility as making possible select practices of knowing and being; that is, through a diffractive reading of such contradictions one might locate onto-epistemological formations that develop within the coming together of individual and class relations and practices: How might different readings of such contradictions make possible entirely new ways of knowing and being that were previously unimaginable? In this case the social justice project takes on productively new dimensionality, one that intra-actively develops and intervenes within such processes. This relational materiality might seek to deterritorialize easy or common sense even as it strives to recognize agential enactments within phenomena—previously unseen interventions that had been blocked by an adherence to the distancing invoked by individualism and/or logics of extraction.

Importantly, to engage in diffractive readings necessarily precludes any *a priori* claims of a subject—there is no "I" before the intra-active relations of phenomena. Thus, inquiry itself is ensconced in the enactment of relational selves, in the production of possible practices of living and knowing that hold the promise of social justice. As a result, individuals are produced—made recognizable—as subjects that adhere to the normative status quo. Subjects are constituted in the very reading/interpretation of events. To borrow from a Deleuzian framework, to engage in diffractive readings is to "plug in" to the very systems in which contradictions manifest and are overcome—phenomena emerge where inquiry connects with material practices. No practices ever go unexamined, just as no examinations ever exist independent of practices. To return to Willis's example of the individual and group, subjects are constituted *as subjects* through the repeated "plugging in" to individualistic values and assumptions of capitalism; conceptions of mobility manifest individually at the contextual moment of this relation. It is through the coming together—the intra-action—of ontology (being), epistemology (knowing), axiology (values), and ethics with material enactments that phenomena develop as events. As such, we can no longer rely solely on external frames with which to square our understandings; instead, we need to develop relational means of inquiry, materially ensconced practices of truth-telling that open up possible futures. Further, the act of truth-telling necessarily disrupts normative function—to tell the truth is to foreclose normative interpretation in favor of previously unimaginable engagements within the world. This is the promise of possibility that is forever emergent within critical inquiry.

Situating social justice inquiry within processes and practices of truth-telling insinuates an ethical component to the production and employment of research, calling forth the notion of *parrhesia* outlined in Chapter 4. Inquiry for social justice from the *parrhesiastic* perspective, like the materialist orientation, emphasizes relational means of knowing, coming to know, and being. In accordance with the orientation of new or critical materialism, *parrhesiastic* inquiry likewise begins with the collapse of knowing, being/living, and ethical practice—an ethico-onto-epistemological orientation. An important element of this collapsed relationality extends from presumptions of necessary relational risk—inquirers need to risk the very relations that define them and give visibility/legitimation to their actions. In this sense inquiry-as-*parrhesia* requires a critical self-reflexivity of the inquirer, as s/he must continually develop truths in relation to multiple and overlapping contexts even as s/he can never fall back on the tentativeness of knowing to refuse assertive truth-claims (this is refusing the risk of truth-telling). In this way the *parrhesiast* is compelled by an ethical dedication toward telling the truth. This determination situates *parrhesia* decidedly within the political realm, foregoing any possibility for "neutral" or "objective" research practices.

Given all of this, how, then, might we reconsider what it means to engage in methodological risk even as we take ownership of a type of methodological responsibility intimated by a materialist approach to inquiry? I have attended to this question throughout this text by asserting particular perspectives on what it means to be methodologically responsible: we saw in Chapter 2 methodological responsibility as one of procedure. Here the methodologist is responsible for enacting the "proper" procedure of method. This is to situate the methodologist as a *technocrat*. Chapter 3 introduced relational ways of knowing and, as such, the methodologist as necessarily revealing the relations through which we construct meaning. This is the beginning of the methodologist as *responsibly materialist*. Lastly, Chapter 4 offered the methodologist as a *materialist truth-teller*. This methodologist necessarily risks him/herself, his/her relations, all in the name of recognizing truth (or making the truth visible) in the name of social justice or progressive social change.

A common criticism of contemporary theoretical work is that it fails the test of prescription. Those who value more extractivist positionings point to a failure on the part of poststructural theory to provide blueprints for next steps. Importantly Foucault (1991) addresses this issue by pointing to the politically important act of critique as resisting the "necessity of reform":

Under no circumstances should one pay attention to those who tell one: 'Don't criticize, since you're not capable of carrying out a reform.' That's ministerial cabinet talk. Critique doesn't have to be the premise of a deduction which concludes: this is what needs to be done. It should be an instrument for those who fight, those who resist and refuse what is. Its use should be in processes of conflict and confrontation, essays in refusal. It doesn't have to lay down the law for the law. It isn't a stage in a programming. It is a challenge directed to what is. (84)

This book, then, is my own "essay in refusal." I want to believe in the possibility for methodological work that refuses the extractivist prerogative. As such, I do not offer specific methodological steps for engaging materialist methodologies but rather a critical orientation that productively affects what it means to act responsibly—to take methodological risks—in our contemporary moment.

Assuming the *parrhesiastic* perspective on truth-telling, one must first consider the very relations through which one gains visibility: What is it that grants me placement in the methodological community? Next, one articulates truths that risk that very relation or identity-formation. Importantly, one does this without fully knowing what this disruption might bring forth, what new relations might form as a result of such disruptive patterning. In this way we necessarily risk ourselves through a dedication to social justice and radical change. This is risky work. Yet what is banded about as "critical" these days is hardly risky; indeed, the distanced critical position may in fact be the safest of them all. This is because much scholarship that proclaims the "critical" mantle does so by maintaining a distance between the critic and what is critiqued. Thus, there is no risk to the critic amidst such distance. Part of this stems, I believe, from a continued adherence to a negative view on power and difference, one that justifies the manufactured distance of critique.

Problematizing Inquiry

Though this may seem an obvious point (especially given the extensive engagement with Foucault's work within the academy), it remains important to recognize the distinctive shift in conceptions of power that extend from Foucault's theorizations and implicate the work of this book. Conceptually I assume this shift from the latter portions of Chapter 2 through this chapter, informing my critique of extractive logic and propelling my belief in inquiry from social change. Rather than power as repressive—as confining or reducing capacity—more contemporary understandings of the term emphasize its productive capacities. As Foucault (1995) writes,

We must cease once and for all to describe the effects of power in negative terms: it "excludes," it "represses," it "censors," it "abstracts," it "masks," it "conceals." In fact, power produces; it produces reality; it produces domains of objects and rituals of truth. The individual and the knowledge that may be gained of him belong to this production. (194)

In line with this thinking and enacted through the chapters of this book, I remain most interested in the productive possibilities of power that may, in turn, affect contemporary notions of methodological responsibility—the many ways in which power makes possible select realities, truth-tellings, identities, and inquiry practices as well as the rationalities that inform them. Further, thinking of power in this way causes me to focus my critical interpretations less on the product (*the* reality, truth-telling, identity, and inquiry practice that results from historical power relations) and more on the formation of such entities—how they come to be within select historical contexts and circumstances. Not *what* but *how* remains the focus of my critique.[3]

This emphasis on *how* aligns with several key elements that drive the theoretical framework of this book: relational and processual analysis, a foregrounded examination of social practices as entry points for social critique, an insistence on a materialist grounding for social critique; and the determined belief that productive social change occurs with renewed understandings for knowing and being—that through *knowing* differently we simultaneously come to be differently. Key to this possibility for social change is a determined shift away from relativism and toward more politically situated practices of inquiry.

As a means to enact all of this, it remains important to extend the productive conceptions of power to its relational capacities. Power is not simply another commodity—a *thing* that someone possesses—but, instead, is produced through the interrelation of individuals, groups, structures, and institutions. As Butin (2001) writes, "Power is not something that some individuals have—such as the sovereign or the police officer—while others do not. Rather, power is embedded in the relations among individuals and groups" (168). Importantly, such a conceptualization of power emphasizes its material impact and production. In this sense power relations are not some abstract formation simply developed through analysis; instead, power relations are identifiable via material actions and practices encountering other material actions and practices—they are made visible through material relation. As a consequence, those analyses that extract lived experiences and practices from their material contexts—that is, those analyses that operate on a *logic of extraction*—necessarily refuse the possibility for resistance in their very dismissal of the material contexts of living.

Re-infusing a critical materiality into inquiry practices, methodological materiality is sustained by an ethical commitment to politically engaged truth-telling. Like Giroux's (2014) appeal for critical educators to intervene in "the dead zone of instrumental rationality" (46), I ask critical inquirers to realign their work and methodological practices with ongoing imaginations for political change in the name of social justice. Admittedly, this involves engaging in ongoing critique of the now (current practices and the logics that inform them) while maintaining a utopic vision of future possibility (practices of living that have yet to be). In this way we might "link critical thought to a profound impatience with the status quo, and connect human agency to the idea of social responsibility and the politics of possibility" (Giroux 2014, 46). Through materialist methodologies as a type of *parrhesiastic* practice, we might allow a collective "impatience with the status quo" to converge with an emergent sense of "social responsibility and the politics of possibility." Through this productive constellation of critical enaction, social change manifests anew. Much like the critical pedagogues who seek to instigate social change through radical education, materialist methodologists see possibilities for changing how we know, act, and become through the very inquiry activities of which we are a part. This is political inquiry as transgressive becoming. Refusing the false disinterestedness of traditional methodological approaches, materialist methodologists embrace *parrhesiastic* visions of telling the truth through a politically engaged process of relational knowing. In this way materialist methodological practices counter the repressive orientation of extractivist methods. At the same time, materialist methodologies critically intervene within the values inherent in neoliberal and globalized processes of knowing and being. This, then, is political work of the utmost importance.

Methodological Activism

By definition, *activism* requires a relational and connective stance. Activism cannot happen in isolation, disconnected or extracted from relation. Hence the ease with which *logics of extraction* dissuade or otherwise make unavailable the very relational thinking required of activism; extractive logics have no room for activist practices. In his description of what he terms the *activist problematic,* Marcelo Svirsky (2010) seeks a definition of activism that is not tied to simply engaging in local struggles but rather draws meaning from "an open-ended process" that "stresses the role of investigation in relation to practices" (163). This link between an ongoing process and investigation into practices remains important to my own conceptualization of activism, methodological responsibility, and inquiry for social change. Importantly, for Svirsky, activism must bring together thought and action and be "present *in* the concept" it seeks to change (166). Notice here the familiar refrain of acting "within" rather than "without"—a perspective shared by critical materialists and activist *parrhesiastic* inquiry. In specific relation to methodology, then, we must understand activism as an integral element of inquiry; conceptually, inquiry necessarily involves activist intent. Much of this intent stems from a determination of the possibility to be otherwise, to no longer foreclose on a future as deterministically defined by the present.

In order to believe in possibilities for activist work, one must have a belief in the openness of the future—that what is to come can never be reducible to the present. As Sharpe (2014) points out, the future always maintains a "constitutive openness" to other formations of being (35). Similarly, our critical reading of the past need not foreclose alternative possibilities that have yet to manifest. Thus, to historicize something is to situate it as an object-of-thought, though not closed off to future changes, irruptions, or possibilities. And yet there are multiple ways in which traditional inquiry practices and processes themselves have come to govern our presumptions about future possibility, creating a determined link between past, present, and future.

As Foucault (1991) asserts, governance entails managing what is (present reality) in order to enable what has yet to be (future realities). Similarly, as Simpson (2012) points out, "one is governed by both reality as it is given and as it can be in the future" (114). Of course, assertions on what is and what might be simultaneously draw from and lay claim to articulations of the past (what noticeably was). As I have shown throughout the chapters of this book, inquiry practices are intimately entwined in this collapse of future and past with the present. As such, critique can only occur through an intense understanding of given reality (how it came to be or is made possible, etc.) with the concurrent refusal to believe that such a reality necessarily extends into the future. This is the work of the critical activist.

Thus, when the *parrhesiast* tells the truth it is a truth-of-the-now, an open-ended belief in how things are with the intention that such a telling might open up the future to unknown—perhaps even unrecognizable—possibilities. In this way the *parrhesiastic* act *intervenes* in the foreclosure of the future—the reductive conflation of *what could be* with *what presently is*. This truth-telling act perhaps begins to consider Denzin and Giardina's (2010) provocative question, "What is the role of critical qualitative research in a historical present when the need for social justice has never been greater?" (15). To answer their question, the authors point to a need for social-justice-oriented intervention:

"As global citizens, we are no longer called to just *interpret* the world, which was the mandate of traditional qualitative inquiry. Today, we are called to *change* the world and to do it in ways that resist injustice while celebrating freedom and full, inclusive, participatory democracy" (17, original emphasis). In order to do so, we might find value in developing a community-based critical capacity for inquiry as social justice work toward a possible future.

How, then, might this implicate contemporary formations of methodological community? As noted throughout this book, methodological expertise is more and more a matter of technical aptitude—the ability to engage and manage a host of increasingly specialized technologies. One might thus consider the implications of the technocratization of methodology (from inquiry to research) as the repeated closure of prescribed boundaries—locating select acts and practices that remain within and those that are positioned on the extraneous margins. Such acts produce communities and prescribed identities (what it means to "be" a methodologist) that are as confining and boundary-claiming as the very technologies that have come to define methodological work (e.g., the recorder or software package).

Following Foucault's (1991) notion of community, formed by required rules regarding procedure and select practices of the self, I understand the methodological community as increasingly determined by an adherence to traditional procedural patterns and rationalities as well as technical ethics of method; bypass the rules, and one potentially loses membership in the community. Of course, the community itself might cease to be, especially within methodological circles, as the role of the methodologist continues to be watered down to technical proficiency, wherein the methodologist takes a backseat to other content-focused specializations.

As critical academics, we have an ethical responsibility to "unsettle power, trouble consensus, and challenge common sense" (Giroux 2014, 52). As Giroux goes on to claim, "Resistance is no longer an option, it is a necessity" (57). In line with contemporary theorizations of relational being and knowing, Patton (2010) situates the activist intellectual *within* the very contexts s/he engages and/or critiques: the intellectual works "within and against the order of discourse within which the forms of knowledge appear or fail to appear. Moreover, [the role of the intellectual] consists of struggling against the forms of power of which he or she is both the object and the instrument" (86). Notice here the refusal of separation between, in this case, the intellectual and that which the intellectual critiques. The intellectual both critiques and is the instrument of reinscription that makes critique possible—and is produced by that which is in need of critique. In order to do so, we methodologists need to engage in ethical practices of discomfort.

As a means for challenging the comfortable position of the educational researcher, Simons, Masschelein, and Quaghebeur (2005) advocate for an experimental "praxis and attitude which is not concerned with 'legitimisation' ... and with defining or defending a 'position', but with 'experience', with experience in the literal sense of 'what is happening to *us*" (827, original emphasis). This is a becoming positionality, what the authors term an "uncomfortable ex-position" that foregrounds a methodological stance of critical becoming and mediates "between past and future ... a position of legitimized limitation and judgment" (827). This might be read as determinedly risky behavior, as the critical methodologist must refuse a position of authority (traditionally established through the expert development and use of norming techniques and technologies) in favor of a more indeterminate location of relational change: "It is an invitation to displace one's gaze" (829). This is a positioning of relation—to oneself, the present, the social world—that exists beyond the level of the epistemological but, instead, within a newly engaged ethical stance of methodological responsibility. As such, this *parrhesiastic* risk involves an openness to giving up one's established positionality, one's identity, within a larger community: "the courage to give up a position and to be engaged in an uncomfortable praxis" (829). Herein lies the productive risk that is essential to *parrhesiastic* practice—*materialist methodologies as activist work*.

From a Deleuzian framework, activist practices are necessarily deterritorializing, making possible new connections, constituting new territories (Svirsky 2010). In this sense activism can nudge previously stable (and normatively reproducing) systems into a state of disequilibrium, thereby intervening in the logical production of the future. This is the interventionist characteristic of activism, a disruptive logic that Svirsky (2010) notes as "hyper-active": "Activism's logic ... first ... [causes] a differential change in the system. Second ... it evaluates each object by causing it to pass through different planes in order to gain critical appreciation of it; at the same time it frees itself from the distractions of habitual recognition that social systems impose upon us" (169). Though perhaps not noted as such, Svirsky's emphasis on causing objects of analysis "to pass through different planes" points to the power of *diffractive* readings—critical analyses that note the contradictions and patterns of difference that emerge through a plurality of interpretive attempts. In this sense the logic that undergirds activist practices is simultaneously critical and disruptive of normative logic formations, those historically reproduced ways of thinking (epistemological assumptions) that have all too often informed our research practices.

There remains an important link between materialists (whether they be of new, critical, or neo-Marxist in order) as I have rendered them throughout this book with implications for activist inquiry practices. Materialists maintain a sustained focus on the daily practices of living and being. In this way my overview of materialisms throughout this book connects with my critique of the *logic of extraction*. This turn to a critique of the everyday sustains my investigation of *parrhesia* and, of course, brings with it particular methodological formations and possibilities. Additionally, conceptions of the relational practices of the everyday link Foucauldian notions of power and subjectification with new materialist claims of the "agential cut" of knowing and being.

Foucault's understanding of processes of subjectification aligns with intra-active considerations: things are not done *to* individuals, but *with* them (Butin 2001). Though perhaps initially seen as a misrecognition of power and agency (certainly, we may want to see individuals as affected by power-laden circumstances or contexts) the shift to intra-actions as productively forming subjects creates renewed possibilities for agency and resistance. This remains an important element for how we engage with participants in our studies. Think, here, of the consequences of (re)presenting individuals as having actions done to them as opposed to with them: such participants become closed subjects, external to the world in which they operate (that which affects them) and have no possibility for reflexively engaging in the very contexts that shape/define them. Agency remains effectively cut off, resistance removed from possibility. Thus, how we understand inquiry—what it is and what it might yet be—becomes an ethical deliberation. Following a Foucauldian perspective, an engaged notion of ethics extends beyond the simple collection of select values or rules toward a relationality—how one relates to one's self—that requires work upon the self (Simons, Masschelein, and Quaghebeur 2005). In this sense *care of the self* requires that one account for oneself, attending to the very relations through which one is known or made visible. Importantly, accounting for oneself, one's relationality, is deeply ethical work—it is to question (and thereby risk) the material relations that grant us meaning. Further still, it is through an engaged ethical stance that one might find resistive pathways to the status quo. As Leask (2011) claims, "ethics ... can provide resistance, or elements of resistance, to the wider regime of governmentality" (8). In this sense it is through ethical deliberation that we might learn to be otherwise, to resist the norming properties of governing structure.

What Is to Be Done?

Time and again students and colleagues who have patiently endured my methodological analyses have turned to the question of: What now? Given the critiques offered to this point, what should one *do*? How can one engage in inquiry during this time of globalized neoliberalism (with the understanding that one can no more step outside the neoliberal context than assert a take-my-ball-and-go-home position of resignation)? How are we to productively engage in methodological work that, in turn, aligns with an activist vision of methodological responsibility to activate some element of social change? What, in short, does it mean to be a responsible methodologist? These are difficult, though no less important, questions. I seek to consider such queries through advocating for a critical methodological community that operates on several activist principles invoking critical inquiry in the name of social change.

Foremost among these principles is a determination to locate our refusal of logics of extraction as a decidedly moral rejection of the social status quo. As noted earlier in this book, ethical considerations are far too often aligned with methodological procedure and, as a consequence, invoked following the articulation of some research procedure; that is, the ethical question is often reductively asked of a study's *implementation.* As materialist methodologists working for social justice, our moral concerns are prior to questions of ethical procedure and/or implementation. For the materialist, moral and ethical assumptions are entangled in questions of being and knowing. Thus, we need to recognize that our claims regarding inquiry are necessarily interwoven within this triumvirate of morality, being, and coming to know. This recognition necessarily alters the daily practices of methodological work even as it clarifies the question of what it means to be methodological responsible in our contemporary context. Bringing a moral sense of responsibility to bear on our methodological work changes our practices: "when method and responsibility collide, it is method that smashes" (Stronach 2010, 165).

To begin, I want to return one more time to an insistence on a collective refusal of an ethically detrimental position of relativism. Postmodern and poststrucutral analyses do not inevitably result in a political paralysis that refuses anything but the most local commentary. As such, we might demand inquiry projects that are overtly politically positioned with an unapologetic stance for necessary social change. And, yes, this stance might certainly begin from an assumed onto-epistemological stance of indeterminacy. Though critics of contemporary social theory might claim a loss of moral positioning as hand-in-hand with indeterminacy, I follow Ian Stronach (2010), who claims a useful strategy of asserting, "it is only in uncertainty that values like justice can be realized" (191, 18). Uncertainty or prescriptive tentativeness need not ultimately lead toward a vacuous ethical or moral stance. Instead, beginning from a place of indeterminacy assumes that social determinations ultimately fail, and it is in that failure that change may occur. Thus it is that our materialist methodological community must begin with assertions of the need for social change, an activist ethic that productively begins from a position of indeterminacy.

Beginning from this indeterminate position requires that our methodological work is *performed* or *performative* (to use Denzin's [2003] language) rather than *representative* of some reality. Representations always inevitably fall short, never fully covering or explaining that which they claim to represent, and stem from a theoretical assumption of determined-knowing that works against materialist methodological stances of activism. Thus, our critical methodological community is one that is performatively engaged, consistently reinterpreting, reconsidering, repairing, and rearticulating claims for needed change at simultaneously local and macro levels. Housed within this performative engagement is a shift from questions of accountability to, instead, engaged ethical deliberation. As Stronach (2010) writes, "a re-articulated world must be governed by ethics rather than accountability, since things are now uncountable, wild, in the wilderness" (169). In many ways, then, our performative inquiry stance is necessarily "governed by ethics": an open-ended ethics toward necessary change, a refusal to recreate *what is to be* as *what has always been.*

In many ways this means responsible methodologists must work against the grain of contemporary contexts and claims on knowing—we necessarily point to indeterminacy and becoming amidst a neoliberal context that most values determined, countable findings. As such, we must devise performative mechanisms for articulating our analyses, ones that open up as much as close off conclusions. This might be seen as an invitation to our readers and one another. Recall here how Lather (2007) and Stronach (2010) both desired readers who actively engage with their texts, having a hand in the production of meaning. This is reading/writing as a relational event. This dialogic engagement aligns well with the *democratic action* required for the types of social-practice-for-social-change through which activism might be performed.

Just as we might assert a need for engaged methodologists—those who refute the reductive positioning of methodologist-as-technocrat—we similarly need to provide openings to engaged readers of our work, engaged members within the communities with which we work, and, more generally, engaged citizens. This again invokes a conception of methodological work as an opening-up of possibility rather than a nailing-down of restricted meaning. To do so is to take seriously the relational meaning-making that extends from the materialist orientation. In short, it is perhaps our responsibility to engage in methodological work that productively affects the world even as we ourselves are open to being affected and changed by the work itself. To do so we perhaps need to reconsider what it means to be critical colleagues engaged in critical methodological communities.

These are, of course, not entirely new claims regarding how we might productively enact a renewed sense of methodological responsibility through relationally engaged materialist methodological work. However, it is, I think, a useful mechanism for reclaiming the role of the materialist methodologist as someone ensconced in risky practices of truth-telling. Following Brian Lord's (1994) assertions regarding the necessary establishment of "critical colleagues" among teachers in the K–12 realm, we might similarly seek out a community that works toward "productive disequilibrium through self-reflection, collegial dialogues, and critique" (192). Here, I want to take Lord's sense of "productive disequilibrium" quite literally: we need to provoke one another to lose our learned orientations within knowing and being, to no longer rely on logics of extraction as an avenue toward reductive clarity. In some ways this is to productively inhibit our learned sense of social proprioception—our tacit understanding of socially material positioning. In so doing, our communal questions might change: questions of "findings" might be exchanged for deliberations of how we "come to claim"; assertions of "what we know" challenged by alternative ways of "coming to know"; displays of "expertise" eschewed by questions of relational citizenship. What remains constant, however, throughout this materialist process is a determination to "tell the truth" of the entangled moment; we reclaim truth-telling in all its tentative, productive power. All of this, of course, is sustained by an energetic activism, a determination to live other than we have, and a collective hope for a more socially just context of the now.

Practically this begins with a methodological shift from "questions of what" to "interrogations of how" (à la Foucault). Aligning material practices with historical assumptions of knowing and being has long been a useful exercise for the criticalist. Indeed, to historicize practices is a first step toward demystifying their common-sensical status within our contemporary context. Yet we are often left without options for the critical shift that extends from *demystifying* practices and assumptions to *dismantling* them, rendering their uncritical enactment impossible in the face of newly relational claims on truth. Within practices of inquiry, this is the strategy of making methodology "stutter"—a goal with which I began this book.

In a similar vein we might draw from a critical or new materialist emphasis on generating diffractive readings of methodological phenomena. As noted earlier in the pages of this book, a diffractive reading emphasizes an experimental, even playful orientation toward meaning—an examination of different patterns of meaning and how knowing might shift given different relational means of coming to know. Inherent in this perspective is a practice of "putting 'oneself' at risk" (Barad 2012, 77): our "selves" are inevitably caught up in the entangled patterns of material relation; to alter such relations is to necessarily alter ourselves. Engaging in diffractive readings of phenomena is to decidedly work against synthesis, against the work of nailing down meaning in favor of a yet-to-be and a yet-to-be-known. The relational opening that comes with a diffractive reading shifts the notion of responsibility away from attempts to claim actions or perspectives as one's own (the misguided assertion that some*thing* or some*one* is "my responsibility") but encourages an opening of responsibility to a relational other (Barad 2012). Responsibility is thus a collective and never fully complete series of relations. We do not get to claim responsibility; we must relationally enact responsibility. And through that responsible enactment we perhaps orient not to justice-as-is but, as Barad (2012) so nicely articulates, a motivation toward "the very question of justice-to-come" (81).

Lastly, recall the symbiotic relation Foucault recognized between *parrhesiastic* truth-telling and democracy. Radical democracy cannot exist without *parrhesia*. Further still, democracy itself is stunted by an overreliance on rhetoric (the façade of truth-telling). As a consequence, to engage in *parrhesia*—to situate inquiry as an act of subversive truth-telling—is a radical democratic act that extends from our own obligations as democratic citizens. Because of our citizenship (in our respective disciplines, in the academy, in our local communities, etc.) we have the right, the obligation to truth-tell, to engage in *parrhesia*. Thus it is that Foucault (2015) notes that truth-telling is "always linked to a practice" (230) and, through its critique of normative thinking, is inherently active. Through this intimate entanglement of democratic citizenship, duty, and truth-telling, *parrhesia* invokes a type of methodological responsibility that requires an engaged activism, one that is necessarily performative. And through the performative, *parrhesia* is always relationally involved: "*Parresia* is always an operation involving two terms; *parresia* takes place between two partners" (240). Further still, it is through the very relational act of truth-telling that the *parrhesiast* opens him/herself to new ways of being and knowing even as s/he critiques traditional formations of coming-to-know. More simply stated, "I am implicated in the truth of what I say" (247). Thus it is that *parrhesia* is a productive truth-telling that, through critical engagement, makes possible a future that is yet to be known.

Conclusion: Methodological Work and Ethical Engagement

I want to conclude with a discussion of ethics—as implied and implicated by extractivist logics and materialist methodologies respectively—as well as considerations for the affective elements of conducting inquiry in our contemporary moment. To begin, I want to consider methodological responsibility and risk according to a Deleuzian framework of an *ethics of immanence,* a relational positioning within the immediate that refuses to consider ethics according to an external square or moral determination that extends beyond present contexts. It remains important to note that situating ethics within an immediate now is decidedly *not* to offer a relativistic ethical positioning (one that I critique in earlier chapters as inadequate and overly simplistic): materialist methodological ethics are necessarily driven by a *relational*—not a *relativistic*—positioning.

As Smith (2007) notes, an imminent ethical positioning emphasizes possible modes of being offered by immediate contexts: "Rather than 'judging' actions and thoughts by appealing to transcendent or universal values, one 'evaluates' them by determining the mode of existence that serves as their principle" (67). In this way ethical evaluation is understood in terms of what is made possible in the moment of enaction. We might remain critical, then, of relations and understandings that separate us from our capacity to act, that remove us from the relations through which we emerge. This is the evaluative engagement that extends from an ethics of immanence.

Inherent in this ethical evaluation is a critical engagement with moral claims to external, extractive frameworks. From external moral positioning stems the "demand to do the impossible" or "the concept of impotence raised to infinity" (Smith 2007, 68). Extractive ethical demands always exceed our immediate moment. Within the grounded context of methodological work we might consider the means by which we are asked to claim absolute ethical stances (e.g., of creating recognizable and interpretable subjects) that inevitably fall short. Perhaps because we can never fully meet extractive ethical demands, we create a host of methodological institutions and apparatuses—such as Institutional Review Boards, checklists for ethical practice, practices such as member checks, and so on—that stand in for ethical deliberation. This is what Denzin (2010) termed "ethics in a cul de sac" (74). Importantly, because these apparatuses and institutions stand outside immediate methodological practice, they cannot anticipate every ethically laden circumstance. In this way extractive ethics have the effect of separating us from our capacity to act in the relational moment, the immediate now.

Following Smith (2007), who notes, "freedom is only for certain acts" (73)—thus causing one to ask which acts do not have to confront the problem of freedom—it is perhaps important to note that methodological responsibility and risk are only for certain methodological acts. In turn, we might ask: Which methodological acts are not confronted with the problems of responsibility and risk? In *logics of extraction* there lie a host of practices that are not required to incur ethical deliberation in the moment of their enaction—they escape questions of responsibility and risk through their very normative placement. Materialist methodologies problematize such practices through situating them within a series of immediate relations, in their immanent production.

In the end, a commitment to inquiry-as-*parrhesia* is an ethical decision, one that takes seriously the relational charge inherent in materialism. Truth-telling from the *parrhesiastic* orientation is inevitably political, recognizing as it does the risky calling-to-question of assumed practices of knowing, living, and being. If we methodologists are to be more than technocratic middle managers, if we are to have a hand in possible social change, we will need to refuse the very extractive rationalities and technologies that grant us our visibility. As Stronach (2010) notes, "it's mad to be sane in a crazy world" (178). Contemporary formations of relational being—as developed in new or critical materialisms have provided the emergent contexts necessary for *parrhesiastic* methodological practice. Ours is thus a time for responsible truth-telling, for opening up the possibility of what has yet to be. This is a decided move away from distrustful claims of impartiality. As Denzin (2010) asserts, ours is no longer a time to dwell in discourses of neutrality:

> Qualitative research ceases to involve learning a set of neutral methodological tools. Inquiry is transformed into moral discourse, a way of being in the world, a way of connecting the inquirer to the worlds of oppression and pain. This means the qualitative researcher must learn a new language, a new way of doing critical inquiry. (62)

What was once highlighted as the gold standard of impartiality, neutral methodological practice is "transformed into moral discourse," an ethically inclined and morally laden sense of activist engagement. This is, indeed, a new methodological language, one productively ensconced in risky truth-telling. Let us not shy away from questions—or even assertions—of truth. Indeed, ours is a renewed responsibility to truth-tell toward a more socially just future. Materialist methodological work as *parrhesiastic* practice.

Notes

Chapter 1

1. I do have doubts, though, on extending this consumerist thinking to solutions meant to stem the momentum of environmental degradation. Creating a "marketplace" for carbon trading, for example, does little to alter the consumerist rationale that contributed to the problem in the first place. As I argue throughout this book, change is needed at the level of logic/rationale; simply creating systems of rationality results in little to no systemic change. Foucault (2008) terms this engaging with codified regimes of truth.

2. One ongoing example of this involves the devaluation of the literature review portion of traditional dissertations to what at times seems a lengthy book report. Instead of engaging with the literature in critical or provocative ways, students invoke what I term the "pointing method" wherein they state what everyone else says without articulating their own thoughtful position; they point to others as a means to point away from themselves. Surely we can establish more critically engaged orientations to the literature that frames our studies.

3. Note also the ease with which this particular presentation of data slips into questions of ownership—this becomes "my data" as though I had some sort of proprietary right to them and/or the meanings that extend from their production. This is data-as-commodity, an issue I address in Chapter 2.

4. Though some might simply say that I am advocating for a participatory-action research approach, I think this categorization is overly reductive. Mine is a relational approach to inquiry that refuses the seduction of the procedural. Relational knowing and coming-to-know *is engaged inquiry*. This is politically minded work that is a necessity given our contemporary times.

5. Many scholars have addressed the role of institutional review boards (IRBs) in regulating inquiry practices within the academy. I, for one, am not strictly against IRBs per se but would rather see them serve as a space for opening up ethical deliberations on inquiry projects rather than shutting them down. Unfortunately, given their disappointing function as procedurizing ethical considerations as well as their placement as the "last word" on whether select projects can, in fact, be undertaken, it would seem that

IRBs most often serve to close down or contain what might otherwise be productive ethical deliberations.

6. Perhaps because I have invoked the term *critical* when describing my own work, I have been asked to speak on several conference panels and symposia dealing with critical methodologies. I have even been asked to participate on a panel dealing with critical quantitative methodologies, though, as I hope my definition of critical makes clear, I have no idea how this particular methodological orientation is even possible (though I am certainly willing to be convinced otherwise).

7. I allude here to a shift from "inter" (between) to "intra" (within) that is characteristic of materialist feminism, particularly the work of Barad (2007). This point is discussed in more detail in my presentation of new materialism in Chapter 3.

8. I have been asked recently, for example, to join a moveon.org petition to stop the slaughter of dolphins, right the injustice of a controversial ending to an Alabama football game, and to deport Canadian singer Justin Bieber from the United States—each of these required the same act and attention from me.

Chapter 2

1. By invoking the term *governmentality*, I here point to Foucault's (2010) use of the term, one that emphasizes "governing" as attempts to shape conduct in particular directions in order to meet particular objectives.

2. Perhaps obviously, this point concerning the role of educational systems in upholding and extending normalized institutions aligns with Althusser's (2014) notion of ideological state apparatuses, insinuating an ideology based on capitalistic notions of production. Thus it is, as Althusser notes, "things and people 'go all by themselves'" (93).

3. For an analysis of new managerialism within higher education, see Aaron Kuntz, Ryan Gildersleeve, and Penny Pasque's "Obama's American Graduation Initiative: Race, Conservative Modernization, and a Logic of Abstraction" (2011).

4. As one anonymous reviewer of this text termed it, this is the "Cresswell Five" approach to research. The phrase, of course, refers to Cresswell's (2012) enormously popular *Qualitative Inquiry and Research Design: Choosing Among Five Approaches.* This text has gained a foothold in introductory methods classes in numerous fields. Its introductory material lends itself to extractive logics, especially considered in isolation from a critically engaged framework for change in the name of social justice.

5. The privileging of such technical markers of validity might be seen in the anxiety enforced by institutional disciplinary mechanisms such as institutional review boards. At my institution I am required to keep transcripts and codebooks under lock and key. Audio files must be destroyed immediately after the production of the transcript. Indeed, the level of procedural detail regarding the handling of such inquiry products is rather astounding.

6. Interestingly, Certeau's notion of "discourse without writing" shares a degree of critical overlap with Karen Barad's (2007) insistence on the mutually constitutive nature of matter and discourse: "Discursive practices and material phenomena do not stand in a relationship of externality to each other; rather, *the material and the discursive are mutually implicated in the dynamics of intra-activity*" (152, original emphasis). Though a systematic explication of the discursive and material is beyond the scope of this chapter, Certeau's notion of how discourse extracts recognizable practices from material contexts is given more dynamic meaning when read against Barad's claims for the material nature of discourse. Barad's articulation of intrarelation is examined more specifically in Chapter 3 in relation to what some have come to term *critical* or *new materialism*.

Chapter 3

1. In *Capital*, Marx (1977) makes this relational point of movement within the context of capitalism. Once capital ceases to move, once it stops its relational flow, it ceases to be capital. We might draw similar conclusions regarding all phenomena as understood from a materialist framework—breaking the relational flow of meaning simultaneously causes phenomena to no longer exist as phenomena. They instead become things, objects that are only simplistically rendered and often misidentified as holding meaning unto themselves (outside relation).

2. Again Marx proves helpful here as he offers the notion of "thingification" (what some theorists term *reification*). Through "thingification" the object of analysis is cut from sociohistorical context and presented as being—or having been—from nowhere. With my colleague John Petrovic, I consider the consequences for citizenship education when *citizenship* becomes a *thing* (Kuntz and Petrovic 2014).

3. The use of the prefix "intra" is intentional here and remains a counter-distinction to the traditional use of "inter" in common parlance. Simply put, "inter" means *between*, whereas "intra" connotes *within*. In this sense, to always remain within select phenomena is to refuse the separateness required of thinking and establishing a "between-ness." To think of *between* requires that one thing be outside relation to another—a dividing recognition I am not comfortable endorsing. Instead, I prefer understandings that are "relations among"—all things relationally known and never fully formed as separate or distinct to one another. For a fuller consideration of how the intra- prefix challenges traditional ways of knowing and meaning-making, see my consideration of Karen Barad's work later in this chapter.

4. An onto-epistemological perspective refuses the distinction commonly established between epistemological (coming to know) and ontological (coming to be) assumptions. As exemplified by Barad (2007), this perspective remains important to my own thinking on truth-telling, methodological responsibility, and inquiry for social justice. Indeed, the first step in productively altering how we engage in critical inquiry

just might be the collapse of the artificial separation between knowing and being/doing. More on this in a bit.

5. As an aside, this desire to exceed itself is perhaps why theorists and philosophers are so (wonderfully? frustratingly?) precise with their word choice—how does one articulate thought and insight in ways that are not hampered by the very logic that informs language? That is, how does one operate outside of the confines of traditional language structure and use the language that is a product of the very rationalities one seeks to critique? Thus, instead of reading theorists such as Foucault or Deleuze as convoluted and needlessly obtuse, we might more charitably understand their project as one that refuses the easy temptation of normative clarity. This would require that the reader, of course, do some work and not simply seek out and operate alongside traditional formations of knowing and coming to know. This explanation is one I often give to students and colleagues alike who complain about the paragraph density of the continental philosophers. With my colleague John Petrovic (2011), I have critiqued this desire for *plain speak* within the context of social theory and educational philosophy.

Chapter 4

1. See David Harvey's (1991) *Condition of Postmodernity.*

2. This leads Deleuze (1990) to take seriously the bemused disorientation endemic in *Alice in Wonderland.*

3. Though this is perhaps an obvious point, I feel compelled to note the ease with which oversimplified renditions of "postmodern theories/analyses" dispute alliances with any truth, thereby paving the way for relativistic claims on meaning and, as a consequence, have little grounding for justifiable claims for social justice work. Notice, of course, that I mentioned this as an oversimplification.

4. This appeal to and simultaneous distinguishing from science as an imagined square against which the merit and worth of inquiry are known continues today. Of course, traditionalist perspectives on inquiry never seem to shake the "physics envy" first identified decades ago. Similarly, we might usefully consider with suspicion the ease with which those who espouse a new materialist approach to inquiry remain enamored with scientific metaphors for meaning. As an example, the work of Karen Barad (2007) has certainly (and rightly so) caught fire within select groups in qualitative approaches to educational research. Barad's onto-epistemological work has affected many methodologists, myself included. At the same time, it does cause one to wonder how Barad's use of physics (of diffractive knowing, etc.) as an example for how "matter comes to matter" in processes of meaning-making perhaps draws on similar desires for inquiry to align with science to thereby generate more interesting/exciting/meaningful interpretations. Admittedly, I am guilty of this as well.

5. As an aside, the critical requirement of academic truth-telling as the interrogation of the values and rationalities of one's peers perhaps makes a strong case for the need

to continue tenure within the academy—a safety net for *parrhesiastic* activity within one's discipline.

6. In recognition of the material reality of this exposure, Lather (2007) recounts in her book an instance of sitting naked in a hot tub while (clothed) colleagues ask her theoretical questions regarding her work.

7. As a colleague of mine is fond of saying, "It's not that schools are broken; it's the opposite. They're too damn good at what they do."

8. This is perhaps why there is such close kinship among methodologists and philosophers—programs of educational research and foundations of education—as they share similar concerns and are similarly political in their pedagogical and scholarly work.

9. It should be noted that there is a useful overlap here between *parrhesia,* from a Foucauldian perspective, and Deleuzian notions of *difference.* Bringing the two approaches together, *parrhesiastic* enactments of truth are perhaps also enactments of *difference.*

10. Though beyond the scope of this chapter, it is nonetheless interesting to note the coincidence of Ian Buchanan's (2014) claims regarding the schizo-society (that of multiple, competing truths all given equal standing, resulting in paralysis) and simplistic recitations of postmodern requirements for a plurality of truths, often disconnected from any material grounding. Again, this is a simplification of postmodern epistemological claims that leads to the accusation of relativism and remains, nonetheless, prevalent within the academy.

11. As an extended example on this, see the ever-growing body of work on the notion of cognitive framing, exemplified by the writings of George Lakoff (2007). A principal aspect of this approach is that the frames themselves carry particular meanings—thus persuasion begins not with the words one uses but the cognitive frames that conjure associations among such words. This line of analysis pushes one disappointingly toward a hyperpolitical *parrhesia* that constructs belief through cognitive manipulation; belief fades into truth.

Chapter 5

1. Of course, it was British Prime Minister Margaret Thatcher who made the most use of the phrase, "there is no alternative" (or TINA). In Thatcher's case, TINA was invoked as a rhetorical mechanism for justifying reforms to enhance liberal capitalism as opposed to changing the system outright. Neoliberal ideologies have further cemented the TINA ideal, assuming that suggestions for possible socioeconomic alternatives are fruitless and naïve; that is, any hope for a more socially just future must assume neoliberal values as a given.

2. Davies's claims here echo St. Pierre's (1997) assertions of our need to "free ourselves" from the "mother tongue" of humanism, examined in Chapter 2.

Notes to Page 131

3. In an interview focusing on his approach to inquiry, Foucault makes a similar distinction between analyzing *what* versus *how*. Specific to his own work, Foucault (1991) notes, "rather than asking *what*, in a given period, is regarded as sanity or insanity, as mental illness or normal behavior, I wanted to ask *how* these divisions are operated. It's a method which seems to me to yield, I wouldn't say the maximum of possible illumination, but at least a fairly fruitful kind of intelligibility" (74, original emphasis). As such, I find most value in discussion regarding *how* we make methodological choices, through better informing *what* such practices entail and *why* they are so easily enacted.

References

Apple, Michael. 2005. *Educating the "Right" Way: Markets, Standards, God, and Inequality.* New York: Routledge.

Althusser, Louis. 2014. *On the Reproduction of Capitalism: Ideology and Ideological State Apparatuses.* Translated by G. M. Goshgarian. New York: London.

Baez, Benjamin. 2014. *Technologies of Government: Politics and Power in the "Information Age."* Charlotte, NC: Information Age.

Barad, Karen. 2003. "Posthumanist Performativity: Toward an Understanding of How Matter Comes to Matter." *Signs: Journal of Women in Culture and Society* 28 (3): 801–31.

———. 2007. *Meeting the Universe Halfway: Quantum Physics and the Entanglement of Matter and Meaning.* Durham, NC: Duke University Press.

———. 2012. "Intra-actions." By Adam Kleinmann. *Mousse* 34: 76–81.

Bennett, Jane. 2010. *Vibrant Matter: A Political Ecology of Things.* Durham, NC: Duke University Press.

Braidotti, Rosi. 2002. *Metamorphoses: Towards a Materialist Theory of Becoming.* Malden, MA: Blackwell Publishers.

Brinkmann, Svend. 2011. "Interviewing and the Production of the Conversational Self." In *Qualitative Inquiry and Global Crises,* edited by Norman Denzin and Michael Giardina, 56–75. Walnut Creek, CA: Left Coast Press.

Buchanan, Ian. 2014. "Welcome Speech." Keynote address at the Deleuze Studies Conference, Istanbul, Turkey, July 14, 2014.

Butin, Dan. 2001. "If This Is Resistance, I Would Hate to See Domination: Retrieving Foucault's Notion of Resistance Within Educational Research." *Educational Studies* 32 (2): 157–76.

Canguilhem, Georges. 1991. *The Normal and the Pathological.* Translated by Carolyn Fawcett. New York: Zone Books.

Cannella, Gaile, and Yvonna Lincoln. 2004. "Dangerous Discourses, II." *Qualitative Inquiry* 10 (3): 165–74.

Certeau, Michael de. 2011. *The Practice of Everyday Life.* Translated by Steven Rendall. Berkley: University of California Press.

Cole, David. 2011. "Matter in Motion: The Educational Materialism of Gilles Deleuze."

Educational Philosophy and Theory 44: 3–17.

Coole, Diana, and Samantha Frost. 2010. "Introducing the New Materialisms." In *New Materialisms: Ontology, Agency, and Politics,* edited by Diana Coole and Samantha Frost, 1–46. Durham, NC: Duke University Press.

Creswell, John. 2012. *Qualitative Inquiry and Research Design: Choosing Among Five Approaches.* Thousand Oaks, CA: Sage Publications.

Davies, Bronwyn. 2010. "The Implications for Qualitative Research Methodology of the Struggle Between the Individualised Subject of Phenomenology and the Emergent Multiplicities of the Poststructuralist Subject: The Problem of Agency." *Reconceptualizing Educational Research Methodology* 1 (1): 54–68.

Deleuze, Gilles. 1990. *The Logic of Sense.* Translated by Mark Lester. New York: Columbia University Press.

———. 1995. *Difference and Repetition.* Translated by Paul Patton. New York: Columbia University Press.

———. 1995. "Postscript on Control Societies." In *Negotiations, 1972–1990,* 177–81. Translated by Martin Joughin. New York: Columbia University Press.

Deleuze, Gilles, and Félix Guattari. 1972. *Anti-Œdipus.* Translated by Robert Hurley, Mark Seem, and Helen Lane. London and New York: Continuum.

———. 1988. *A Thousand Plateaus: Capitalism and Schizophrenia.* Translated by Brian Massumi. Minneapolis: University of Minnesota Press.

DeMartino, George. 2013. "Ethical Engagement in a World Beyond Our Control." *Rethinking Marxism* 25 (4): 483–500.

Denzin, Norman. 2003. *Performance Ethnography: Critical Pedagogy and the Politics of Culture.* Thousand Oaks, CA: Sage Publications.

———. 2010. *The Qualitative Manifesto: A Call to Arms.* Walnut Creek, CA: Left Coast Press.

Denzin, Norman, and Michael Giardina. 2010. "Introduction." In *Qualitative Inquiry and Human Rights,* edited by Norman Denzin and Michael Giardina, 13–41. Walnut Creek, CA: Left Coast Press.

———. 2014. "Introduction." In *Qualitative Inquiry Outside the Academy,* edited by Norman Denzin and Michael Giardina, 9–31. Walnut Creek, CA: Left Coast Press.

Derrida, Jacques. 1983. "The Principle of Reason: The University in the Eyes of Its Pupils." *Diacritics* 13 (3): 2–20.

Desjarlais, Robert. 1997. *Shelter Blues: Sanity and Selfhood Among the Homeless.* Philadelphia: University of Pennsylvania Press.

Foucault, M. 1983. "On the Genealogy of Ethics: An Overview of Work in Progress." In *Michel Foucault: Beyond Structuralism and Hermeneutics,* edited by Hubert Dreyfus and Paul Rabinow, 231–32. Chicago: University of Chicago Press.

———. 1991. "Questions of Method." In *The Foucault Effect: Studies in Governmentality,* edited by Graham Burchell, Colin Gordon, and Peter Miller, 73–86. Chicago: University of Chicago Press.

———. 1995. *Discipline and Punish.* Translated by Alan Sheridan. New York: Vintage

Books.

———. 1997. *The Politics of Truth.* Translated by Lysa Hochroth and C. Porter. Los Angeles: Semiotext(e).

———. 1998. "Polemics, Politics and Problematizations." In *Essential Works of Foucault,* edited by Paul Rabinow, vol. 1 of *Ethics,* 111–19. New York: New Press.

———. 2001. *Fearless Speech.* Los Angeles: Semiotext(e).

———. 2003. *Society Must Be Defended: Lectures at the College De France: 1975–1976.* Translated by David Macey. New York: Picador.

———. 2007. *Security, Territory, Population: Lectures at the College De France: 1977–1978.* Translated by Graham Burchell. New York: Picador.

———. 2008. *The Birth of Biopolitics: Lectures at the College De France: 1978–1979.* Translated by Graham Burchell. New York: Palgrave MacMillan.

———. 2010. *The Government of Self and Others: Lectures at the College De France: 1982–1983.* Translated by Graham Burchell. New York: Picador.

———. 2011. *The Courage of the Truth (The Government of Self and Others II): Lectures at the College De France 1983–1984.* Translated by Graham Burchell. New York: Palgrave Macmillan.

———. 2015. "*Parrhesia.*" Translated by Graham Burchell. *Critical Inquiry* 41 (2): 219–53.

Frankfurt, Harry. 2009. "On Truth, Lies, and Bullshit." In *The Philosophy of Deception,* edited by Clancy Martin, 37–48. New York: Oxford University Press.

Geertz, Clifford. 2001. *Available Light: Anthropological Reflections on Philosophical Topics.* Princeton, NJ: Princeton University Press.

Gibson-Graham, J. K. 2003. "An Ethics of the Local." *Rethinking Marxism* 15 (1): 49–74.

———. 2014. "Being the Revolution, or, How to Live in a 'More-than-Capitalist' World Threatened with Extinction." *Rethinking Marxism* 26 (1): 76–94.

Giroux, Henry. 2014. "Public Intellectuals Against the Neoliberal University." In *Qualitative Inquiry Outside the Academy,* edited by Norman Denzin and Michael Giardina, 35–60. Walnut Creek, CA: Left Coast Press.

Harvey, David. 1991. *The Condition of Postmodernity: An Enquiry into the Origins of Cultural Change.* New York: Wiley-Blackwell.

———. 2001. *Spaces of Capital: Towards a Critical Geography.* Routledge: New York.

Hunter, Ian. 1994. *Rethinking the School: Subjectivity, Bureaucracy, Criticism.* Sydney, Australia: Allen & Unwin Publishers.

Kenway, Jane, and Anna Hickey-Moody. 2011. "Life Chances, Lifestyle and Everyday Aspirational Strategies and Tactics." *Critical Studies in Education* 52 (2): 151–63.

Kincheloe, Joe, and Peter McLaren. 2005. "Rethinking Critical Theory and Qualitative Research." In *The Sage Handbook of Qualitative Research,* 3rd ed., edited by Norman Denzin and Yvonna Lincoln, 303–42. London: Sage Publications.

Kisby, Ben. 2014. "Citizenship Education in England in an Era of Perceived Globalization: Recent Developments and Future Prospects." In *Citizenship Education Around the World: Local Contexts and Global Possibilities,* edited by John Petrovic and Aaron

Kuntz, 1–22. New York: Routledge.

Kuhn, Lesley. 2008. "Complexity and Educational Research: A Critical Reflection." *Educational Philosophy and Theory* 40 (1): 177–89.

Kuntz, Aaron. 2011a. "Science, Health, and Nationhood: Methodological Pathology in an Era of Conservative Modernization." *International Review of Qualitative Research* 4 (3): 199–218.

———. 2011b. "The Work of the Criticalist: Critical Civic Literacy and Intervention in Class Processes." In *Critical Civic Literacy: A Reader,* edited by Joe Devitis, 169–79. New York: Peter Lang.

———. 2015. "Critical and Poststructural Forms of Inquiry: Social Justice Through Productive Critique." In *Critical Qualitative Inquiry: Foundations and Futures,* edited by Gaile Cannella, Michelle Perez, and Penny Pasque, 113–38. Walnut Creek, CA: Left Coast Press.

Kuntz, Aaron, and John Petrovic. 2011. "The Politics of Survival in Foundations of Education: Borderlands, Frames, and Strategies." *Educational Studies* 47 (2): 174–97.

———. 2014. "Reading Citizenship Education in Neoliberal Times." In *Citizenship Education Around the World: Local Contexts and Global Possibilities,* edited by J. Petrovic and A. Kuntz, 237–52. New York: Routledge Press.

Kuntz, Aaron, and Marni Presnall. 2012. "Distancing the Interview: Coming to Sense in Material Intra-action." *Qualitative Inquiry* 18 (9): 732–44.

Kuntz, Aaron, Ryan Gildersleeve, and Penny Pasque. 2011. "Obama's American Graduation Initiative: Race, Conservative Modernization, and a Logic of Abstraction." *Peabody Journal of Education* 86: 488–505.

Lakoff, George. 2007. *The Political Mind: Why You Can't Understand 21st-Century American Politics with an 18th-Century Brain.* New York: Viking Press.

Lather, Patti. 2007. *Getting Lost: Feminist Efforts Toward a Double(d) Science.* Albany: State University of New York Press.

Leask, Ian. 2011. "Beyond Subjection: Notes on the Later Foucault and Education." *Educational Philosophy and Theory* 44: 1–17.

Lemke, Thomas. 2011. "Critique and Experience in Foucault." *Theory, Culture, Society* 28 (4): 26–48.

Lincoln, Yvonna, and Gaile Cannella. 2004. "Dangerous Discourses: Methodological Conservatism and Qualitative Research." *Qualitative Inquiry* 10 (1): 5–14.

Lord, Brian. 1994. "Teachers' Professional Development: Critical Colleagueship and the Role of Professional Communities." In *The Future of Education: Perspectives on National Standards in America,* edited by Nina Cobb, 175–204. New York: College Entrance Examination Board.

Marcus, George, and Michael Fischer. 1999. *Anthropology as Cultural Critique: An Experimental Moment in the Human Sciences.* Chicago: University of Chicago Press.

Marx, Karl. 1977. *Capital: A Critique of Political Economy,* vol. 1: *Capital: A Critique of Political Economy.* Translated by Ben Fowkes. New York: Random House.

Mazzei, Lisa, and Alecia Youngblood-Jackson. 2009. "Introduction: The Limit of Voice."

In *Voice in Qualitative Inquiry: Challenging Conventional, Interpretive, and Critical Conceptions in Qualitative Inquiry,* edited by Lisa Mazzei and Alecia Youngblood-Jackson, 1–13. New York: Routledge.

McLaren, Peter. 1995. *Critical Pedagogy and Predatory Culture: Oppositional Politics in a Postmodern Era.* New York: Routledge.

Olssen, Mark, and Michael Peters. 2005. "Neoliberalism, Higher Education and the Knowledge Economy: From the Free Market to Knowledge Capitalism." *Journal of Education Policy* 20 (3): 313–45.

Papadopoulos, Dimitris. 2010. "Activist Materialism." *Deleuze Studies* 4: 64–83.

Pasque, Peny, Rozana Carducci, Aaron Kuntz, and Ryan Gildersleeve. 2012. *Qualitative Inquiry for Equity in Higher Education: Methodological Implications, Negotiations, and Responsibilities.* San Francisco: Jossey-Bass.

Patton, Paul. 2010. "Activism, Philosophy, and Actuality in Deleuze and Foucault." *Deleuze Studies* 4: 84–103.

Pearce, Cathie, and Maggie MacLure. 2009. "The Wonder of Method." *International Journal of Research and Method in Education* 32 (3): 249–65.

Peim, Nick. 2009. "Thinking Resources for Educational Research Methods and Methodology." *International Journal of Research and Method in Education* 32 (3): 235–48.

Pillow, Wanda. 2003. "'Bodies Are Dangerous': Using Feminist Genealogy as Policy Studies Methodology." *Journal of Education Policy* 18 (2): 145–59.

Resnick, Stephen, and Richard Wolff. 1987. *Knowledge and Class: A Marxian Critique of Political Economy.* Chicago: University of Chicago Press.

Rice, J. A., and Michael Vastola. 2011. "Who Needs Critical Agency?: Educational Research and the Rhetorical Economy of Globalization." *Educational Philosophy and Theory* 43 (2): 148–61.

Roberts, Peter. 2014. "Tertiary Education and Critical Citizenship." In *Citizenship Education Around the World: Local Contexts and Global Possibilities,* edited by John Petrovic and Aaron Kuntz, 220–36. New York: Routledge.

Rosaldo, Renaldo. 1993. *Culture and Truth: The Remaking of Social Analysis.* New York, Beacon Press.

Ross, Alison. 2008. "Why is 'Speaking the Truth' Fearless? 'Danger' and 'Truth' in Foucault's Discussion of *Parrhesia.*" *Parrhesia* 4: 62–75.

Rudolph, John. 2014. "Why Understanding Science Matters: The IES Research Guidelines as a Case in Point." *Educational Researcher* 43 (1): 15–18.

Sharpe, Scott. 2014. "Potentiality and Impotentiality in J. K. Gibson-Graham." *Rethinking Marxism* 26 (1): 27–43.

Simons, Maarten, Jan Masschelein, and K. Quaghebeur. (2005). "The Ethos of Critical Research and the Idea of a Coming Research Community." *Educational Philosophy and Theory* 37 (6): 817–32.

Simpson, Zachary. 2012. "The Truths We Tell Ourselves: Foucault on *Parrhesia.*" *Foucault Studies* 13: 99–115.

Smith, Daniel. 2007. "Deleuze And The Question of Desire: Toward An Immanent

Theory Of Ethics." *Parrhesia* 2: 66–78.

St. Pierre, Elizabeth. 1997. "Circling the Text: Nomadic Writing Practices." *Qualitative Inquiry* 3 (4): 403–18.

Steele, Brent. 2010. "Of 'Witch's Brews' and Scholarly Communities: The Dangers and Promise of Academic *Parrhesia*." *Cambridge Review of International Affairs* 23 (1): 49–68.

Stronach, Ian. 2010. *Globalizing Education, Educating the Local: How Method Made Us Mad*. London: Routledge.

Svirsky, Marcelo. 2010. "Defining Activism." *Deleuze Studies* 4: 163–82.

Wacquant, Loic. 2004. *Body & Soul: Notebooks of an Apprentice Boxer*. Oxford: Oxford University Press.

Willis, Paul. 1977. *Learning to Labor: How Working-Class Kids Get Working-Class Jobs*. New York: Colombia University Press.

Youngblood Jackson, Alecia, and Lisa Mazzei. 2012. *Thinking with Theory in Qualitative Research: Viewing Data Across Multiple Perspectives*. London: Routledge.

Index

About the Author

Dr. Aaron M. Kuntz is department chair of Educational Studies and an associate professor at the University of Alabama. He serves as program coordinator for the PhD in educational research and teaches graduate courses in qualitative inquiry and foundations of education. As an engaged and collaborative scholar, Dr. Kuntz develops inquiry projects in local, national, and international arenas alongside professional colleagues, teachers, and community activists. Dr. Kuntz's research agenda focuses on theorizing and developing "materialist methodologies"—ways of producing knowledge that take seriously the theoretical deliberations of critical theory, postmodernism, and poststructuralism that have emerged in social theory over the past fifty years. He grounds this methodological theorizing in empirical questions about the production of inquiry in the K–16 arena, faculty work, and activism in postsecondary institutions and the impact of the built environment on learning. His research interests include critical qualitative inquiry, academic activism and citizenship, critical geography, and philosophy of education. Kuntz's publications appear in such diverse journals as *Qualitative Inquiry, Cultural Studies↔Critical Methodologies, Journal of Language and Politics, Journal of Higher Education, Review of Higher Education, International Journal of Qualitative Studies in Education, Higher Education Policy,* and others. He coauthored *Qualitative Inquiry for Equity in Higher Education: Methodological Implications, Negotiations, and Responsibilities* (Jossey-Bass) and coedited the volume *Citizenship Education: Global Perspectives, Local Practices* (Routledge). He received his doctorate in education from the University of Massachusetts Amherst.

Made in the USA
San Bernardino, CA
15 August 2018